The Billings Method

Using the body's natural signal of fertility
to achieve or avoid pregnancy

Dr Evelyn Billings
& Dr Ann Westmore

NEW EDITION 2003
Reprinted 2004

First published in 1980
by Anne O'Donovan Publishing Pty Ltd
GPO Box 5073, Glenferrie South, Vic. 3122

Reprinted 1980, 1981
New edition first published in paperback 1982
Reprinted 1982, 1983, 1984 (twice), 1985, 1986, 1987
New edition 1988
Reprinted 1990
Revised and reset 1992
Reprinted 1993, 1994, 1995
New edition 1997
Revised 1998, 2000
Revised and reset 2003
Reprinted 2004

Cover design by Beth McKinlay
Illustrated by Pam Brewster
Set in Palatino by Midland Typesetters, Maryborough, Vic.
Printed and bound by Griffin Press

National Library of Australia
Cataloguing-in-publication entry

Billings, Evelyn, 1918– .
 The Billings method: using the body's natural sign of fertility
 to achieve or avoid pregnancy.
 New ed.
 Bibliography.
 Includes index.
 ISBN 1 876026 42 1.
 1. Birth control. 2. Natural family planning – Ovulation method.
 3. Ovulation – Detection. 4. Cervix mucus. 5. Contraception.
 I. Westmore, Ann, 1953– . II. Title.
613.9434

Published with the approval of

World Organisation/Ovulation Method/Billings

Distributed in Australia by
Penguin Books Australia Ltd

Contents

THE BILLINGS METHOD . . .

'The book will be of major interest to the
many millions throughout the world who for
any reason—personal, cultural, religious,
ecological or medical—do not want to use
hormones, chemicals or devices for birth control.'
—*Professor John Bonnar, University of Dublin*

'Offers hope and advice for those
interested in family planning—
either to have or not to have.'
—*Hugh R. K. Barber, MD,*
Director, Department of Obstetrics and
Gynaecology, Lenox Hill Hospital,
New York City

'The Billings Ovulation Method is the
safest and most effective method so far
available for fertility regulation.'
—*Professor S. Z. Qian,*
Jiangsu Family Health Institute, China

Preface

Since the first appearance of this book more than two decades ago, the Billings Method has enjoyed increasing acceptance, not only among the general public but also in scientific circles, where the research studies of Professor James B. Brown of Melbourne, Australia, and Professor Erik Odeblad of Umea, Sweden, have made an impressive impact. The self-knowledge that comes to a woman from keeping a daily record of her mucus signal of fertility is becoming recognised by medical practitioners as a valuable diagnostic tool.

Professor Brown's Ovarian Meter, the culmination of a lifetime's study of ovarian function, enables a woman to measure oestrogen and progesterone accurately throughout her cycle. While not ordinarily necessary, it has proved to be a valuable adjunct to the method in circumstances of difficulty due to organ pathology or temporary readjustment of hormonal patterns. It enhances the confidence of women, and will assure doctors of their ability to interpret the changing mucus patterns of fertility and to identify the time of maximum fertility and ovulation. It also shows that a woman can identify an unchanging mucus pattern that indicates infertility.

Since 1968, when the method was first taught, by invitation, outside Australia, official teaching has been established in more than a hundred countries through the efforts of many teachers from Australia and other parts of the world. A considerable spread of knowledge has followed teacher-training, one-to-one instruction of couples and international conferences. Extensive scientific research and successful field trials have supported this activity. Teaching methods have become simpler: illiteracy is now no barrier to teaching or learning.

Recognition of both the fertile patterns of cervical mucus and the infertile patterns of discharge is unique to the Billings Method. For many years the guidelines of the method have remained unaltered. Initially they were formulated with the help of couples themselves, then later verified by hormonal monitoring. Professor Odeblad, after some half a century of research into the structure and function of cervical mucus, explained the mucus patterns and their significance in relation to sperm function and conception, thus providing further verification. His explanation of the role of the vagina in producing normal discharges associated with conditions such as breastfeeding, and their relation to the patterns of ovarian hormones, confirmed the concept of the unchanging nature of the Basic Infertile Pattern. Of particular value has been his contribution to our knowledge of post-Pill infertility. Professor Brown has travelled extensively, lecturing on the hormonal basis for the method. The influence of Professor Odeblad in the Scandinavian countries, and his setting up of teacher-training programs there, extended the work greatly.

We first visited China in 1986 in order to undertake a program organised by the State Family Planning Commission of China. Subsequently the method was established in Jiangsu Province in The Nanjing Billings Natural Fertility Regulation Method Research Centre of Excellence. The program was enhanced by an Australian Government grant for the period 1995–98 for additional work in Anhui Province, directed from Yiji-Shan Hospital, Wannan Medical College in Wuhu City. This resulted in women being trained as teachers in several teaching programs in collaboration with the Provincial Family Planning Commission. The method has been acknowledged as an acceptable option within the State (national) Family Planning Program.

We continue to participate in training seminars in China. The adverse effects of technological methods of birth control are well known to Chinese doctors, who speak freely about them and are very ready to consider a natural alternative. Acceptance of the scientific proof of the Billings Method is now commonplace. In Nanjing alone, there are more than 2000 trained teachers of the method, and 20 000 couples have been taught; of these, 10 000 are ready to proceed to accreditation as teachers. Similar centres of teacher-training are proceeding in over half of China's provinces and major cities.

Trials of the Billings Method in China, India, Indonesia and North Africa among poor illiterate people of diverse religions—Hindus, Muslims and Christians—or of no religion have revealed a method effectiveness of more than 99 per cent when it is used according to the guidelines. Government bodies responsible for population control acknowledge the efficacy of the method and the obvious health and social benefits accompanying its use. The Billings Method is capable of providing a real solution to the problem of population control, needing no expensive technology, and requiring only normal medical care to deal with abnormalities.

The system of teacher-training around the world has led to an enormous increase in the use of the Billings Method. By 1987 a survey through the teaching centres revealed that at least 50 million couples were involved. Since the method is easy to learn and teach, it has a natural spread from mother to daughter and woman to woman. Its application in alleviating infertility, and in predetermination of the sex of the baby, has contributed to its proliferation. Of particular significance is the teaching of young adults, whose appreciation makes this a particularly worthwhile enterprise.

Women who have read this book have been able to teach themselves the method and enjoy the satisfaction of self-knowledge and command of their fertility. Couples who adopt the Billings Method find that co-operation with the gentle discipline strengthens their bond: as a woman of Cameroon commented to us, 'This method is love'.

The future of the method lies in careful teaching and preservation of the authentic, scientifically verified guidelines. This depends on teachers who are dedicated to helping other people as they themselves have been helped, teachers who have been enriched by a simple solution to what has often been a desperate problem for couples.

Evelyn L. Billings,
March 2003

Acknowledgements

Acknowledgement is due to the following people.

To the Rev. Fr Maurice Catarinich, who by his perseverance and analytical questioning was responsible for much of the early development of the method. His kind and wise counselling, especially in the field of infertility, is invaluable.

To the scientists, especially Professor James B. Brown, who during several decades of close association has provided hormonal monitoring of women's observation of cervical mucus, in collaboration with Dr Patricia Harrisson and Dr Meg Smith. His research work continues. He has performed some 800 000 hormonal analyses which continue to verify the women's observations in all circumstances.

To Professor Henry G. Burger who, working with Professor Brown, established the hormonal correlations with the Peak symptom and the beginning of the fertile phase, thereby producing irrefutable evidence of the validity of the method. He also read the manuscript of the original book, and later editions, and has offered many helpful criticisms.

To Professor T. Hilgers (USA); to Professor R. Blandau (USA) for the unique photographs from his library; and to Professor E. Odeblad (Sweden) for permission to use his illustrations and include his invaluable research findings.

To the thousands of teachers around the world of all races and creeds who, seeing the benefits of the method, have been faithful in preserving its orthodoxy and tirelessly teaching it. I would like to thank particularly those many

Australian teachers some of whom have been involved in this work for up to thirty years and have visited many other countries. Some have accompanied us, over more than ten years, in visits to China and other countries.

During this time refinements to teaching techniques have developed especially due to the vision and industry of Marie Marshell of Melbourne, which have been enthusiastically adopted and applied by many others in disseminating the work. It is impossible to name individually all those who have assisted us to continue this work, among them many doctors, medical scientists, missionaries, and other advisers, including couple users.

To financial benefactors, without whom we could not have travelled so extensively nor assisted the establishment of teaching centres, particularly in the under-privileged countries.

To our Education Committee, on whom falls the essential task of monitoring teaching materials, worldwide training of teachers, running doctors' courses and publicity, as well as teaching all who ask. Their services are unpaid except in the currency of gratitude.

To Mercedes Wilson, who devised the coloured-stamp system of charting, and for her photographs in this book.

To Anne O'Donovan, whose clear concept of the book was achieved with meticulous care, and whose generosity enabled the book to appear in some countries with publishing difficulties.

To Dr Ann Westmore, who exhibited good humour, patience and skill in writing the book, and to her son Michael, who contributed much to the pleasure of our early collaboration.

To Pam Brewster, whose drawings of scientific data very cleverly combined accuracy with beauty; to Margaret Barrett and, more recently, Sarah Dawson, who have edited the various editions; to Beth McKinlay, who designed the new cover; and to Alison Forbes, who designed the text.

*To Dr John Billings who, responding to the needs
of couples, recognised the practical value of the
cervical mucus as a natural sign of fertility.
He showed women how to solve their fertility
problems by self-knowledge and encouraged
them to teach other women.*

CHAPTER 1

What is the
Billings Method?

Throughout history women have sought to control and
manage their fertility.

Many primitive methods have been used. And enormous expenditure has been directed towards chemical
and mechanical methods of contraception. However, the
magnitude and severity of side-effects of pills, injections,
intra-uterine devices and implants are increasingly
apparent. Many women have turned away from the Pill
because of its wide-ranging effects on the body.

Sterilisation is widely practised. But many couples find
this an unacceptable approach to fertility control. They see
a vacuum, which has not been filled by natural techniques
such as the Rhythm and Temperature methods, which
have been found to be both unreliable and restrictive.

Conscious of this gap, Dr John Billings began work on a
simple yet substantial theory: that women themselves can
recognise when they are fertile or infertile by the characteristics of the discharge which they can feel and see at the
vaginal opening. Recognising the importance of the
mucus as a marker of fertility was a finding of remarkable
significance. A group of Melbourne doctors and medical
researchers has spent the last forty years developing and
researching an easily understood, accurate and scientific

system which would allow this dramatic piece of knowledge to be be used by any woman.

The basis of the method is awareness of the mucus. This mucus can indicate, by its sensation and appearance, your pattern of fertility. It is produced by the cervix, which is the part of the uterus that joins with the vagina, and which is under the control of the reproductive hormones. Scientific research has shown that not only does the mucus signal the fertile state, it also appears to be essential if conception is to take place. For without the mucus, sperm transport is impeded and the sperm cells die quickly in the acid environment of the vagina.

When the mucus indicates possible fertility it is necessary to postpone sexual intercourse if a pregnancy is not desired. For most couples, this means that up to half the days of a typical cycle are available for intercourse. In general, days available for intercourse are grouped throughout the cycle so that abstinence is not required for lengthy periods in any cycle. If a couple wants to have a child, the method can help them to achieve this. Indeed, many women experiencing difficulty becoming pregnant have found success by being attentive to the mucus that indicates fertility and timing intercourse to coincide with it.

This method, now known as the Billings Method, is a natural method in that no drugs or devices are needed— just a simple awareness of the changing mucus and the application of this knowledge. It is as effective, properly used, as any other known method of fertility control. The scientific facts are indisputable. The research background to the method is set out in chapter 15. Like some other methods, it is susceptible to the human factor, but couples who are motivated to make it work will find it safe, reliable and simple to use. A few cycles are usually all that is necessary before confidence in the method is assured. A daily record is essential.

Many women have discovered the significance of the mucus themselves, and have used it as a sign of their fertility or infertility even without the scientific verification of the method that is available today. For instance, it is known that at least three African tribal groups (the Taita, Kamba and Luo) have used the mucus produced by the cervix as a marker of fertility for generations past. And an elder of an Australian Aboriginal tribe, Niranji, has described how young girls of his tribe were taken away to a sacred place by the older women and taught about the mucus. In western societies, it is not unusual to hear of an individual woman who has discovered for herself the message of the mucus.

The reliability of the method was further demonstrated by an early World Health Organisation trial in five countries. Findings indicated a method effectiveness of 97 per cent or better. This means that among 100 couples *who followed the method guidelines* for a year, three pregnancies or fewer were expected to occur. More recent trials have reported effectiveness greater than 99 per cent, exceeding that of modern contraception and sterilisation. The WHO trial results also showed that over 90 per cent of women can produce a recognisable chart of their mucus after only one cycle.

We know that teaching quality affects the success rate significantly. Most women will be able to learn the method from this book, but some will also find it helpful to consult a trained teacher with whom questions and unusual circumstances can be discussed. A list of the teaching centres is given at the back of the book.

Anyone who wishes to make a success of this method can do so. The motivation and co-operation required enhance the relationship. Successful use calls for partners to act in accordance with the signals of fertility and infertility. This means, for example, that you will need to show your love in ways other than intercourse sometimes.

Natural family planning seems to work best when couples are clear about whether they want to have a child. Some are ambivalent about this and test the fertile time by deviating from the guidelines. They will not be surprised when pregnancy follows. Acceptance of the baby as their loving responsibility is engendered by this method, which puts couples in full possession of their reproductive possibilities. The method appeals to couples who feel that fertility control is a joint responsibility and that because of this, neither partner should be required to bear a health burden.

The Billings Method is applicable to all phases of a woman's reproductive life—whether her menstrual cycles are regular or irregular, during adolescence, coming off the Pill, when breastfeeding or approaching the menopause. Each of these special situations is described in a later chapter of the book.

The method causes no side-effects; the natural body processes are not disturbed. This can be an awakening for women who have been using contraceptive medications which alter normal hormone patterns and which can cause irritability, depression, nausea, loss of libido, and sometimes more serious pathological disorders. Couples are also free of any possible aesthetic objections to using devices such as condoms, diaphragms and IUDs. With this method no equipment is necessary; all the information you need to regulate your fertility comes from your own recognisable patterns of fertility and infertility. A bonus of the method is the sense of wonder and deep satisfaction that comes from tuning in to the natural rhythms of your own body.

The method also provides a valuable guide to your gynaecological health. Menstrual cycle irregularities need no longer be a mystery. If an abnormality develops, your mucus will alert you to the problem at an early stage, when treatment is most likely to prove effective.

Women's dissatisfaction with all other known methods of contraception can be heard throughout the world. We have only recently come to realise that Nature herself has provided the answer. The recognition of these fertility signs is like remembering something about ourselves long forgotten.

After reading this book, you will be able to:
- recognise the signs of fertility and infertility
- apply this information and skill to suit your needs
- experience the benefits of the method in terms of satisfaction, happiness, and improved communication with your partner.

CHAPTER 2

The mucus discovery

Once, the only natural family planning method available was the Rhythm Method.

This method is based on the finding that ovulation occurs, on a single day, eleven to sixteen days before menstrual bleeding starts. This gives a woman with near regular cycles a means of calculating the days when she is most likely to be fertile. Basing her calculations on the shortest and longest cycles experienced over six to twelve months, she can work out the range of days of possible fertility.

The Rhythm Method is satisfactory as long as cycle length does not change markedly. But it has an inherent fault. No woman is always regular. Inevitably there are significant variations in cycle length—caused by emotional or physical stress, after a pregnancy, or close to the menopause.

The Rhythm Method proved unreliable and needlessly limiting especially when cycles were long and irregular. This is the natural pattern for some women and does not call for corrective treatment unless an underlying abnormality is present. But women with such cycles need to be able to interpret them if they are to be in command of their fertility.

Clearly what was needed was a marker of fertility that women themselves could recognise. With this in mind, Dr John Billings made a search of the medical literature in 1953. To his surprise—not being a gynaecologist—he found several accounts of a stringy lubricative mucus, produced at about the time of ovulation by the cells lining the cervix.[1,2,3,4]

Although this mucus had been observed by doctors for many years, to his knowledge gynaecologists had never questioned women about their awareness of it. Indeed, as early as 1855, Smith[5] had stated that conception was most likely to occur when the mucus was 'in its most fluid condition'. Sims[6] in 1868 likewise pointed out the importance of the mucus when he first described the post-coital test for sperm health, saying that it should be carried out when the mucus becomes 'clear and translucent and about the consistency of white of egg'. In 1913, Huhner[7] further investigated Sims's work, and confirmed the desirability of a particular type of mucus for the Huhner's test (described on p. 149). Experiments by Seguy and Simmonet[8] in France in 1933 involving laparotomy, where the ovary is viewed directly, confirmed the time of ovulation and accurately related this to the mucus with fertile characteristics and to the peak of the hormone oestrogen.

John Billings recognised the possible significance of the mucus as a marker of ovulation. Could the mucus with fertile characteristics be used as a signal of fertility? After questioning a small number of women, it became clear that the occurrence of different types of discharge during the menstrual cycle was a familiar observation. It then became a matter of determining whether a typical pattern existed during the cycle, and whether women could identify their fertile phase.

With the co-operation of hundreds of women, a standard mucus pattern quickly emerged. It became evident, despite some individual variations, that the sensation produced by the mucus, as well as its appearance, could enable *all* women to recognise the onset of fertility. Even blindness proved to be no barrier to learning. And the pattern appeared similar for women in different societies. (This was confirmed in the 1970s by the five-nation World Health Organisation trial.)

My involvement in research and teaching the method began in 1966. It quickly became clear that woman-to-woman teaching was the most effective way of getting the message across. The basic problem for men who have tried to teach the method is that they can never experience ovulation and therefore only dimly appreciate the observations and sensations of the cervical mucus that provide the key to successful use of the method. Additionally some women find it difficult to talk freely about the mucus to a male teacher.

By the mid-1960s a prolonged clinical study of the mucus had been completed, and a set of guidelines formulated for fertility control. At this stage, only the mucus pattern associated with ovulation, and the infertile phase following it, had been identified. Rhythm calculations were still used to deal with the first part of the cycle. This was inadequate for women with irregular cycles or delayed ovulation, such as those approaching the menopause or breastfeeding a baby. However, it became apparent that many women familiar with the method found it unnecessary to take their basal body temperature and were ceasing to do so. They found that the mucus changes alone gave adequate information: that in some women the change from a pattern of dryness to one of mucus signalled fertility; in others a change from a pattern of continuous, unchanging mucus to any mucus that was different, also signalled fertility.

The recognition of the infertile patterns of either dryness or mucus before ovulation, was at the same time a fascinating discovery and a tremendous relief because it disposed of prolonged abstinence. As long as the discharge or dryness that a woman correctly identified as her infertile pattern remained unchanged, intercourse could not result in conception. Each step along the way to establishing reliable and universally applicable guidelines for fertility control was tested many times and correlated with hormonal studies. The unchanging pattern before ovulation corresponded with a basic low hormonal level and was thus called the Basic Infertile Pattern.

In 1971, temperature measurements and Rhythm calculations were discontinued. The Billings Ovulation Method, now refined and validated in many studies, could stand alone for all circumstances of reproductive life. Mothers, knowing whether they were fertile or infertile, could continue to breastfeed their babies. No longer was it considered necessary to wean the baby so that ovulation would occur. Women approaching the menopause could now recognise with confidence their extended phases of infertility, free from anxiety, and the long wait for a rise in temperature that might never occur again.

Opposition to the Billings Method came from those who confused it with the Rhythm Method, or who lacked the correct information and expertise to teach it successfully. This opposition stimulated the continued scientific investigations and field trials that established beyond doubt the validity of the method. Scientific research into the method initially involved hormonal studies, where a profile of the various hormones involved in reproduction can be obtained from very sensitive measurements. Participants in hormonal studies included women with normal cycles, nursing mothers, pre-menopausal women, and those with cycle disorders such as failure of ovulation, disturbed mucus pattern, and women having difficulty conceiving. Investigations of the method also involved studies of the characteristics of the cervical mucus during the fertile and infertile phases of the cycle. This research helped many infertile couples to achieve a pregnancy. In more recent years, the techniques of ultrasound and laparoscopy—where the changes occurring on the surface of the ovary can be viewed directly—have been used.

These and other research projects are described in detail in chapter 15, which sets out the scientific basis of the method.

> The laboratory studies of the mucus, the laparoscopic data, the hormonal assays and the infertility research have all provided confirmatory evidence that a woman's own awareness provides an extremely accurate guide to her state of fertility.

In the following chapters, the practical implications of the mucus discovery are spelt out . . . the 'how', 'when' and 'why' of using the Billings Method.

CHAPTER 3

Getting to know your menstrual cycle

The possibility of conceiving a child in any menstrual cycle is limited to a short sequence of fertile days. This fertile phase is usually about five days in a typical cycle, which averages twenty-three to thirty-five days in length.[1]

Cycles shorter than twenty-three days, and very long cycles of more than thirty-five days, occur from time to time in most women, but the fertile phase remains approximately constant. Mucus quantity may vary.

Irregular cycles are much more common at the two extremes of reproductive life—adolescence and middle age—than during the years from about twenty to forty. Menstrual irregularities are also common after weaning a baby, or when coming off the Pill.

It is natural for some women to be very irregular and normally fertile. They require no regulating treatment. The Billings Method works equally well whether cycles are regular or irregular.

The phases of the menstrual cycle

THE BLEEDING PHASE—MENSTRUATION   The number of days of menstrual bleeding in each cycle is commonly four or five, although the reported range is wide. At the beginning

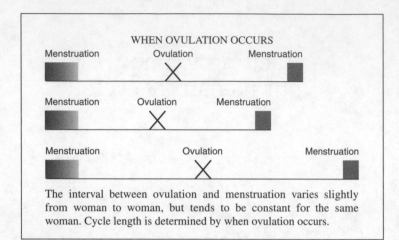

The interval between ovulation and menstruation varies slightly from woman to woman, but tends to be constant for the same woman. Cycle length is determined by when ovulation occurs.

of the days of bleeding, which is taken as the start of the menstrual cycle, the ovaries—which are the oval-shaped organs within which the egg cells mature—are at a low level of activity. At this time of the cycle only small amounts of the female hormones oestrogen and progesterone are circulating in the blood-stream.

THE PRE-OVULATORY PHASE   As a result of this low-level ovarian activity, the hypothalamus, a walnut-sized collection of highly specialised brain cells, sends out a chemical message, known as a hormone, to the pituitary gland at the base of the brain.

Pituitary hormones which act on the ovaries are triggered. Several nests of cells called follicles, each containing a primitive egg, start to develop within the ovaries, and produce a hormone of the oestrogen group known as oestradiol. This is the hormone which activates the cervix to produce mucus, the substance that appears at the vaginal opening and signals the state of fertility.

Usually only one of the follicles in the ovary reaches full maturity in a cycle. The others, having been active for

THE HORMONE MESSAGE SYSTEM BETWEEN THE BRAIN, THE OVARIES, THE UTERUS AND MUCUS PRODUCTION IN THE CERVIX

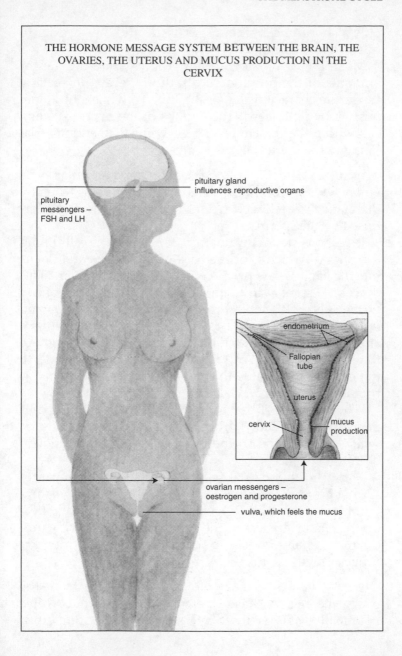

pituitary gland
influences reproductive organs

pituitary
messengers –
FSH and LH

endometrium

Fallopian
tube

uterus

cervix

mucus
production

ovarian messengers –
oestrogen and progesterone

vulva, which feels the mucus

only a short time, become scar tissue and they appear to fulfil no further function.

Meanwhile the developing follicle releases larger amounts of the hormone oestradiol, thereby increasing the fertile characteristics of the mucus, while simultaneously moving towards the surface of the ovary. The egg cell within the follicle is also growing. The endometrial lining of the uterus begins to grow.

OVULATION   There is only one day in any particular cycle when ovulation occurs. Ovulation is the process whereby the egg cell is released from the ovary, ready to be fertilised by the sperm.

In response to oestradiol from the ovary, the cells lining the cervix—which is at the base of the uterus and opens into the vagina—are producing a very special mucus. This mucus is essential in maintaining the fertilising capacity of the sperm. It enables sperm movement by providing guiding channels and a protective environment for them, and sustains them nutritionally during their journey to the Fallopian tubes. And it captures damaged sperm. All the evidence indicates that unless this special mucus is produced by the cervix, *conception cannot take place.*

When the egg cell leaves the follicle, the remaining cells develop into a yellow structure called the corpus luteum which produces the hormone progesterone, in addition to oestradiol.

These hormones cause the lining of the uterus to further grow and thicken to provide nutrition in preparation for a pregnancy. Progesterone has a profound effect on the characteristics of the mucus from the cervix producing a change which a woman can herself identify. Progesterone also increases the body temperature.

THE POST-OVULATORY PHASE   After its release from the ovary, the egg cell has a life-span of only about twelve hours unless it is fertilised by a sperm cell. The numerous

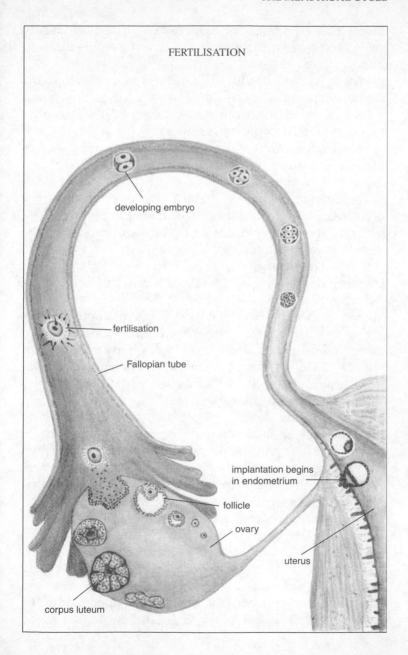

FERTILISATION

developing embryo

fertilisation

Fallopian tube

implantation begins
in endometrium

follicle

ovary

uterus

corpus luteum

finger-like fronds at the wide end of the tube gently sweep the surface of the ovary so that the egg is directed into the tube.

Within its twelve-hour span it starts to move along the funnel-shaped Fallopian tube towards the uterus, aided by wave-like contractions of the tube and the brushing motion of microscopic hairs lining it.

Fertilisation—the union of an egg and a sperm—takes place in the outer third of the Fallopian tube, *less than a day after ovulation.*

The final stage of the maturing of the egg does not occur until after fertilisation. This fact is reassuring since it demonstrates the vitality of the egg and precludes the development of an old egg.

When the sperm membrane fuses with the outer covering membrane of the egg, the cell, called a zygote (which means 'yoked together', and which is the earliest human embryonic body), now springs into activity and, given the correct conditions, will grow and develop during a life-span of some seventy or eighty years. When the sperm and egg fuse, the inherited characteristics of the new individual, such as hair colour, physique, and biochemical make-up, are established.

While rapidly developing, this embryo travels along the tube and at about six days begins to embed in the nourishing lining of the uterus, called the endometrium. Implantation is complete by twelve days after ovulation.

The growth of the nutritive endometrium is stimulated by both oestrogen and progesterone, the continued secretion of which is assured by the hormones produced by the implanting embryo. In any cycle, the time during which the endometrium is thickened and filled with nutrients suitable for receiving the developing embryo is only about thirty-six hours. Precise correspondence between stages of development of the fertilised egg and the endometrium is essential for successful implantation.

If the egg is not fertilised it dies and disintegrates. And about fourteen days later (the range is from eleven to sixteen days), the endometrium breaks away resulting in menstruation. This shedding of the endometrium occurs when the levels of the hormones oestrogen and progesterone decline.

The process of menstruation has been likened to a tree shedding its leaves in winter: with the next cycle, new growth begins again. New follicles develop, oestrogen is released, and a new endometrium grows in readiness for a possible pregnancy.

Sometimes bleeding occurs without an egg cell being released. This is termed anovular bleeding. Such cycles are more common around the time of puberty and at the menopause, when hormone levels are insufficient to cause the egg to be released.

However, under the influence of oestrogen, the lining of the uterus still grows, and is shed with bleeding when the level of the hormone declines.

Other changes during the menstrual cycle

The hormonal events of the menstrual cycle cause psychological as well as physical changes which vary from woman to woman. Most women are aware of altered moods and physical characteristics corresponding to different stages of their cycle. Emotional peaks and troughs both immediately before and during menstruation have been documented, ranging from irritability, depression, anxiety and fatigue, to elevated mood states.

It is common for breast tenderness and lumpiness to precede menstruation, and this may cause feelings of discomfort. Some women report migraine headaches during the first day or two of bleeding. Lower abdominal pains bear a variable relationship to ovulation.

Around the time of ovulation, the mucus at the vaginal

opening undergoes significant changes. This mucus—produced by the cervix—provides the key to recognising your fertility. It will be discussed in more detail in the next chapter.

By developing an awareness of the events of the menstrual cycle and especially the changes in the mucus, women can learn to recognise their fertility or infertility with precision, and plan their lives accordingly.

The lymph node sign

Due to increased lymphatic drainage about 70 per cent of women notice an enlargement and tenderness of a small gland (node) in the groin, a day or two around ovulation. The gland enlarges on the same side as the ovary that is ovulating. Vulval swelling is often more marked on the side where the gland is felt.

The woman makes this examination by lying down and placing her hands over the groins with her fingers pointing to her toes. If the middle finger is resting over the leg artery, whose pulse can be felt, the index fingers will be in a position to feel the pea-sized tender lump. A daily examination will enable the woman to assess the development of the node and determine the side on which she is ovulating. This may have a practical application when, due to Fallopian tube damage, she may wish to delay conception until ovulation occurs on the side of the healthy tube and so avoid the possibility of an ectopic pregnancy.

This lymph node sign was discovered by Professor Erik Odeblad in his research in Sweden.[2]

CHAPTER 4

The key to fertility control—
the mucus

When the ground is dry a seed will not germinate. But when the rains come prepare for a harvest. So it is with a woman, that when she is wet with the mucus and for three days afterwards she may expect the harvest of a baby.
—Teaching the Billings Ovulation Method in the World Health Organisation study, El Salvador, central America.

We usually represent the menstrual cycle as beginning with the menstrual bleeding and ending as the next period of bleeding starts. In a fertile cycle, you ovulate on one day only. Even when two eggs develop (as happens with twins) both are released on the same day. If no pregnancy occurs, your menstrual bleeding will start about two weeks after ovulation.

The sensation of wetness associated with menstruation is often your first indication of a period. So it is with the mucus.

Sometimes during your cycle you wonder if a period has started. You feel something wet and slippery outside the vagina. When you check, you see a white, or clear, stretchy mucus. You may think—'Oh well, that's nothing'. But far from being nothing, this mucus—the fertile mucus—is a most important sign of good health and fertility. It is produced by the cells of the cervix for an average of six days before ovulation.[1]

Mucus with fertile characteristics appears to be essential for fertility. Both clinical and laboratory studies have shown that the most fertile time in the cycle coincides with mucus with fertile characteristics, and that infertility is associated with an unchanging pattern lacking fertile characteristics.

This mucus provides the sperm cells with a protective envelope so that the sperm retain their fertilising capacity for three days, and occasionally for as long as five days (but only if mucus is present). Without it, sperm cells deteriorate rapidly: even minutes in the normally acid environment of the vagina will cripple sperm.[2]

The essential mucus nourishes the sperm cells by supplementing their energy requirements and, in some way not yet fully understood, may make the sperm cells capable of fertilising the egg. The mucus acts as a filter, destroying damaged sperm cells (every ejaculate contains a proportion of these) which are removed by scavenger cells in the area.

As well as providing protection and nourishment, the mucus also forms guiding channels which help the sperm to move along the vagina, through the cervix and uterus, and into the Fallopian tubes. Even mucus outside the vagina can enable sperm cells to reach the egg. (Thus pregnancy can result following genital contact without full penetration taking place.)

While learning to recognise the patterns of discharge that indicate fertility or infertility, it is important to keep a daily record of your observations.

Do not be concerned that your pattern does not conform to that of other women. Episodes of mucus with fertile characteristics may be longer or shorter in duration and the mucus may be more or less in quantity. Each woman will find that she has her own recognisable pattern which is as individual as she is.

THE SPERM AND THE MUCUS

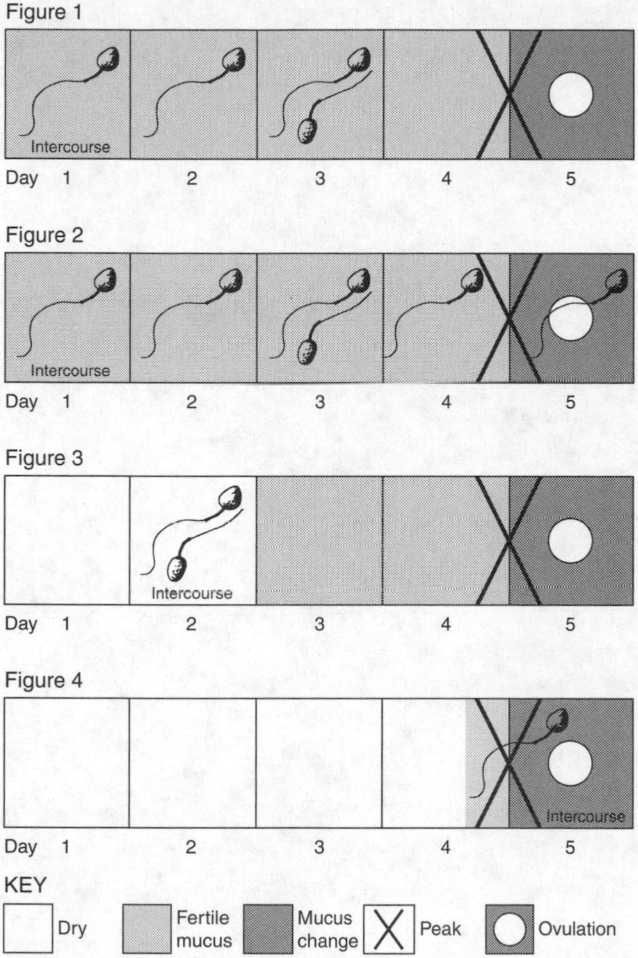

Figure 1

| Day | 1 | 2 | 3 | 4 | 5 |

Figure 2

| Day | 1 | 2 | 3 | 4 | 5 |

Figure 3

| Day | 1 | 2 | 3 | 4 | 5 |

Figure 4

| Day | 1 | 2 | 3 | 4 | 5 |

KEY

☐ Dry   ▨ Fertile mucus   ▨ Mucus change   ✕ Peak   ◯ Ovulation

Sperm usually retain their fertilising capacity for three days (Figure 1), but under optimal mucus conditions, occasionally for up to five days (Figure 2). If intercourse takes place on a dry day (Figure 3), sperm fertilising capacity is quickly impaired. If intercourse occurs on or just after the Peak (Figure 4), conception is most likely.

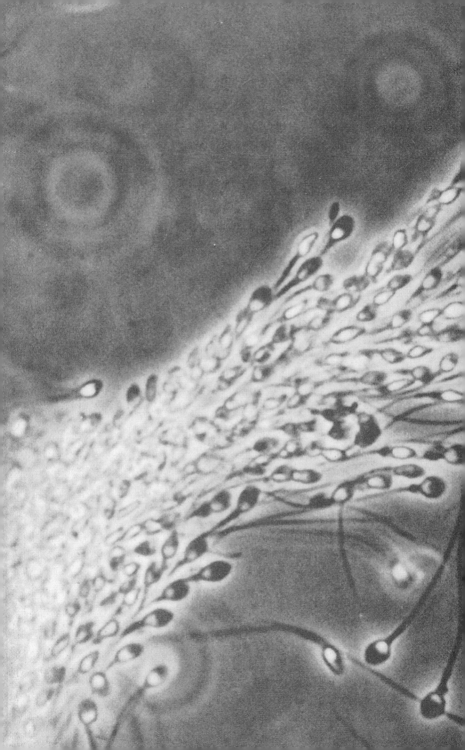

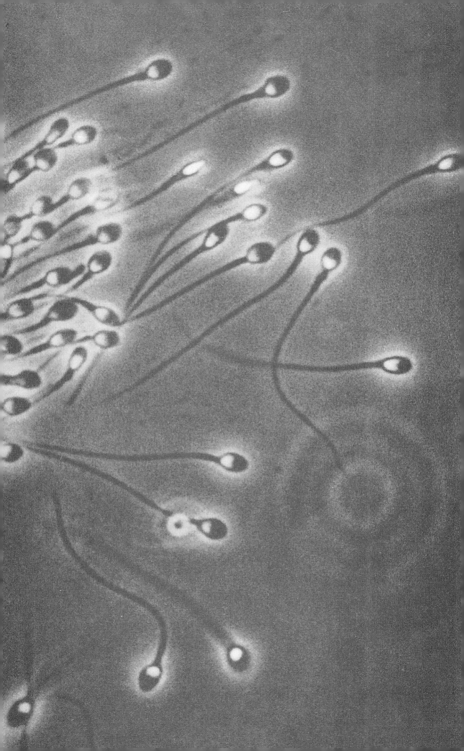

Watch for changes in the sensation and appearance of the mucus. These are the vital indicators of altered fertility. Do not assess fertility or infertility by an isolated mucus sample. For example, sticky mucus may begin the fertile phase after dryness. It marks a change.

Most women quickly grasp the pattern of their fertility, but a trained teacher will ensure that you are correctly interpreting your record.

While learning the method it is necessary to avoid intercourse during the first two to four weeks of recording. This enables you to gain a clear picture of your mucus pattern. It is possible for seminal fluid or vaginal secretions associated with intercourse to confuse the picture while you are getting to know your mucus pattern.

What sort of pattern can you expect?

The Basic Infertile Pattern (BIP)—the unchanging pattern

In one common type of cycle, the sensation you experience after your menstrual bleeding is dryness. No mucus is seen or felt, and this is described as a *Basic Infertile Pattern of dryness.*

In the other common pattern, there are no dry days after menstruation. Mucus is visible, and it is usually dense, flaky, and scant in amount. It may produce a sensation of stickiness or dryness. And it continues day after day *without change of any kind.* This unchanging mucus is described as a *Basic Infertile Pattern of mucus.*

In a typical twenty-eight day cycle, a BIP of dryness or of mucus, one or the other but not both, lasts for two to three days or longer after the menstrual bleeding.

While dry days can be determined during the first month of charting, several cycles may be necessary to interpret with confidence the BIP of mucus, and the point of change.

The photograph on the previous pages shows sperm moving through the fertile mucus (*Dr R. Blandau*).

The pattern of fertility—the changing pattern

The first indication of the change leading to ovulation may be sticky thread-like mucus after dry days, or a feeling of moistness after a succession of sticky days.

These sensations are experienced on the skin outside the vagina. You may see a lump of cloudy mucus that has been resting like a plug in the cervix. As the days pass, you will notice that the mucus becomes thinner, clearer, more profuse, and then merely slippery.

Women use all sorts of expressions to describe the fertile characteristics of the mucus—looping, like strings of raw egg-white, smooth or slippery. It may be clear, cloudy, or tinged with blood, in which case it may look slightly pink, brown, red or yellow. It will always have a wet, slippery property because of its chemical structure and composition, even when there is too little to see (diagram, p. 211).

A characteristic odour of the fertile mucus is familiar to many women. This has been noted particularly by the blind.

The fertile phase begins, with a change from the BIP, on average six days before ovulation. For however many days the mucus is present, it provides ample warning of the approach of ovulation and the need for absolute avoidance of intercourse and genital contact if a pregnancy is not desired . . . for sperm are kept alive and healthy by mucus with fertile characteristics.

The sensation and appearance of mucus with fertile characteristics may be accompanied by a feeling of fullness, softness, or swelling in the tissues around the opening of the vagina. It's like a ripening—something which many women can associate clearly with fertility. No other signs of fertility, such as pain or spots of blood, are as precise or reliable as the mucus.

When the general vaginal region is lubricated by this

fertile mucus, libido and interest in lovemaking may be heightened. Mistakenly, some women think that sexual desire produces the secretion.

The Peak of fertility

The last day of any of the fertile characteristics of the mucus—that is, the last day when it looks stringy or stretchy or produces a sensation of lubrication without visible mucus—is the *most fertile day* of the cycle.

You will know it is the last day only in retrospect. This day is called the Peak of fertility, because it is the day when intercourse is most likely to result in a pregnancy. It is important to realise that it is not necessarily the day of *most mucus*. This is a common error.

The key to the Peak is that it is the *last day of any of the mucus with fertile characteristics*—that is, the last day when the mucus at the vaginal opening looks stringy or feels lubricative. The lubricative sensation may last a day or two longer than the appearance of strings of mucus, indicating that you are still highly fertile. The sensation is the most valuable sign. Some women will see no mucus.

Studies show that ovulation usually occurs within a day of the Peak mucus signal (p. 210). A World Health Organisation trial indicated that over 90 per cent of women can identify the fertile phase and the Peak day of fertility in the first month of observation. Encouragement and practice can further increase this figure. The occurrence of a menstrual period approximately two weeks after your recognised Peak will confirm your observations and your confidence will grow with succeeding cycles.

The small number of women who cannot identify a recognisable mucus pattern require special assistance; they may need to be particularly alert to the sensation that the mucus produces outside the vagina. Sometimes only a small amount of mucus is produced and sensation

THE FEMALE REPRODUCTIVE SYSTEM SHOWING THE EFFECT OF THE MUCUS ON SPERM MOVEMENT

biological valve closed – pre-ovulatory phase

Fallopian tube

follicle

ovary

uterus

cervix

mucus plug impenetrable to sperm

biological valve open – ovulation

fertilisation

about 200 normal sperm cells reach the egg. abnormal cells are filtered out by the mucus in the cervix

fertile mucus forming pathways and protection for sperm

mixture of normal, old, immature and abnormal sperm cells (about 300 million)

will be the prime guide. This is important for a woman having difficulty conceiving.

A few women will find it difficult at first to believe that reliable signs of fertility are available and will think they have no mucus. They may have dismissed any chance observations of wetness as due to intercourse or stimulation, or even to infection.

Do not be discouraged. By being alert to the changing sensations that even a minute quantity of mucus produces, you will soon learn your own signs of fertility.

If you are having difficulty in determining your fertile phase, daily temperature measurements for a few cycles may prove helpful in indicating whether you are ovulating or not. The Ovarian Meter is more accurate (see p. 215).

The post-ovulatory phase

In a typical cycle, the time between ovulation and the beginning of menstruation is about fourteen days. This interval tends to remain constant for the individual.

For three days following the Peak signal, you should watch the characteristics of your mucus very carefully. If the wetness or slipperiness return within three days of a doubtful Peak, this suggests that ovulation has been delayed.

When ovulation has occurred, the discharge will become sticky, cloudy, and dry for the rest of the cycle. Or it may stop completely. When complete dryness or this sticky, dry mucus has continued for three successive days past the Peak, it can be assumed that ovulation has taken place, and that the egg cell is dead.

CHAPTER 5

Keeping your mucus record

The most effective way of learning to recognise your mucus signals is to record your observations daily on a chart. The aim is to identify on any day whether intercourse could or could not result in pregnancy. You will be ready to use the method after observing for one month.

For quick, easy reference, a set of coloured markers has been devised to record observations. At first, observations are made using only red, green and white stamps or coloured pencils. These are interpreted by study for two to four weeks. After this learning stage the mucus patterns can be identified and recorded as infertile or possibly fertile. Always observations, not interpretations, are recorded.

Keeping a record of your mucus becomes second nature. It merely requires that you attach the appropriate sticker to the chart every evening, and add a few words to describe the sensation produced by the mucus outside the vagina, and its appearance, during the day. Charts and stamps are available from the centres listed at the back of this book. If you are unable to obtain these, you may wish to devise your own chart or photocopy the one provided at the back of this book.

Several different systems of recording cycles have been

BILLINGS METHOD COLOUR CODE

RED for days of bleeding or spotting.

GREEN where no mucus is observed and there is a sensation of dryness.

WHITE for mucus that is possibly fertile.

YELLOW for infertility, that is, discharge that remains the same, day after day after day before ovulation. This can be recognised as indicating infertility after studying a cycle or two. Thereafter the yellow stamp means infertility and the white stamp means possible fertility. Yellow stamps are also used for mucus after ovulation. These days are infertile because the egg is dead.

---

invented. Buttons of different shapes are strung on a string by the blind. Teachers in developing countries have adapted the method to meet the needs of the local community. Women in parts of India tie knots in a rope looped around the waist; in other countries information is scratched on the trunk of a tree; women in Papua New Guinea thread coloured beads or flowers on a string.

Daily recordings help you to become familiar with your mucus patterns in normal cycles; when stress delays ovulation; and in altered reproductive circumstances—such as when a pregnancy is desired, or during breastfeeding, or when approaching the menopause. Typical examples of charts while learning the method, and for long and short cycles, are illustrated in Figures 1, 2 and 3 (p. 130).

The first and most important step in learning the method is to develop an awareness of the mucus and its changes.

If your mucus signs are unclear, it may be helpful to

discuss them with a Billings Method teacher. There are now many such teachers throughout the world. For information write to your nearest Billings Method Centre.

If you are ovulating rarely, for instance while approaching the menopause, or if you have not ovulated since the birth of a child, you can learn to recognise your Basic Infertile Pattern after keeping a chart for about two weeks. *Any change from this pattern signals a possible return of fertility.*

During the initial month while learning to assess your mucus signals through charting, it is recommended that you do not have intercourse and avoid all genital contact, including withdrawal. Barrier contraceptive devices, such as condoms or diaphragms, should not be used, for the pattern of cervical mucus may be obscured by seminal fluid or vaginal secretions released during sexual activity.

Many women discontinue daily charting when they are confident of their ability to interpret their mucus accurately. However it is advisable to continue to keep a record of your mucus, if there is a serious reason to avoid pregnancy.

How do you observe the mucus?

SENSATION The mucus produces a sensation on the skin outside the vagina. This is the more important observation. As you go about your normal activities you may be aware of a sensation of wetness, stickiness or of nothing at all (dryness).

Even a very small non-visible quantity of mucus can change the sensation from dry to not-so-dry, sticky, moist, slippery, or wet. Some women will be discouraged if they expect to see mucus which looks like clear raw egg-white and which stretches without breaking.

APPEARANCE At any time you feel the presence of the mucus you can note its appearance. Women have their own individual ways of doing this.

A woman learns to evaluate her own observations which are personal to her. A consistent routine of making observations is recommended.

If there is sufficient mucus to be seen and collected, it can then be checked for clarity, stretchiness, blood staining, thickening, colour changes, stickiness, glueyness, blobs and lumps, and changes in quantity.

The fluidity of highly fertile mucus causes it to stretch easily and ensures its presence outside the vagina very soon after its production in the cervix. You do not need to examine the inside of the vagina. It is always moist, and thus confusion is likely to result.

Very tight undergarments may sometimes make it difficult to feel the sensations outside the vagina. Since these sensations are extremely important indicators of your state of fertility, it is preferable to wear underclothes that are sufficiently loose to enable you to tune in to your sensations. The use of absorbent panty liners may alter the sensation. Vulval swelling is a significant sign of high fertility.

When do you check the mucus?

There is no particular time of the day. Most women using the method automatically make a mental note of any mucus when they go to the toilet. They are also alert for sensations around the vaginal opening at any time.

Use your own words when, at the end of every day, you note down the sensations and appearance of the mucus, particularly the most fertile sign that you have experienced during the day.

Your description need not mean anything to others. Simply record your mucus observations without trying to interpret them at first. Women who say that they neither feel nor see any mucus are often surprised at what they notice once given basic information about what to look for. They often produce a classic pattern at the first attempt.

In a new situation, such as when breastfeeding or approaching the menopause, it is advisable to resume charting. In such circumstances, infertility may be the dominant state and Peaks of fertility may occur only occasionally or not at all; *recognition of infertility* is now the key to controlling your fertility.

One important bonus of keeping a chart for some couples is that it may open up areas of discussion about intimate and vital matters including fertility regulation. For the method demands communication about emotions and sexuality, and this often enhances a relationship.

Some men like to see the chart so that they can accommodate themselves to its requirements. For instance, they will know whether it is desirable or undesirable to have intercourse at a particular time of the cycle, if the intention is to avoid a pregnancy. In this way, they can give support and assurance to their partners about following the guidelines.

This joint approach to fertility control is in line with the growing awareness that the combined fertility of both partners at any particular time determines whether or not a pregnancy occurs. The sharing of responsibility for a pregnancy lifts the burden of fertility control from one partner, and encourages an attitude of mutual and responsible loving that is the foundation of successful and intelligent family planning.

When are you fertile?

The length of the fertile phase depends on the combined fertility of yourself and your partner. That is, it depends on the rapid transport and maintenance of the fertilising capacity of the sperm (typically two or three days and occasionally up to five days)—which is directly related to the presence of fertile cervical mucus—as well as the time of release of the egg and its subsequent survival (typically the egg lives for about twelve hours).

The guidelines described in the next chapter provide a built-in safety margin to minimise the possibility of an unplanned pregnancy.

CHAPTER 6

Applying the method— the guidelines

In these guidelines, abstinence from intercourse includes the avoidance of all genital contact. This is because healthy sperm cells can move from outside the vagina to the Fallopian tubes when fertile-type mucus is present. In this way an unintended pregnancy may occur.

When intercourse is inadvisable, don't give up loving altogether.

'We have found a limitless set of possibilities in our sexual relationship, since using the Billings Method. Sexuality is loving, understanding, touching, being close, and exploring a vast range of shared experiences.'

Guidelines to avoid a pregnancy

THE EARLY INFERTILE DAYS—THE EARLY DAY RULES   The early infertile days are the days before any change occurs. These days may be dry, without any sign of mucus; or you may have mucus which, be it flaky, sticky or dense, remains the same day after day after day.

Both these patterns are referred to as a Basic Infertile Pattern (BIP)—the first is a BIP of dryness; the second a BIP of unchanging mucus. Both indicate that you are infertile. A *change* in either indicates possible fertility.

Intercourse should be confined to the evenings in the early part of the cycle so that the Basic Infertile Pattern can be confirmed during the day. Otherwise a change to the mucus with fertile characteristics may occur during the night, and you and your partner—unaware of your increasing fertility—may have intercourse in the morning which could carry some possibility of a pregnancy.

Intercourse on alternate days will provide greater safety, because seminal fluid and vaginal secretions tend to obscure the mucus on the day following intercourse. Twenty-four hours is sufficient for the seminal fluid to disappear completely.

If your BIP is dry days, and these are interrupted by a day of mucus or bleeding, it is advisable to avoid intercourse on these days and for three days afterwards. This three-day margin allows the pattern to become either possibly fertile or obviously infertile. If the BIP of dryness returns without recognition of the Peak, once again alternate evenings are available for intercourse from the fourth BIP evening.

If the BIP is days of continuous unchanging discharge and this is interrupted by days when the mucus has changed or bleeding occurs, once again avoid intercourse on these days and for three days afterwards. If your BIP of discharge returns you may safely have intercourse on alternate evenings. The BIP occurs before the Peak only.

FERTILE DAYS—THE PEAK DAY RULE   Any *change* in the amount, colour, consistency or wetness of the mucus indicates some activity in the ovaries, and the possibility that you are fertile.

Postpone intercourse as soon as any change from your BIP is observed or felt. Continue to avoid intercourse during the days of change until the Peak is identified. The

Peak is the last day of a sensation of lubrication or the appearance of any clear or stringy mucus. It coincides closely with swelling of the vulva and ovulation (see chapter 15).

THE PEAK RULE   Intercourse is available from the beginning of the fourth day past the Peak until the end of your cycle. These Late Infertile Days are the days when the combined fertility of you and your partner is zero. Ovulation is over and the egg is dead. Once the Peak has been identified correctly no abstinence is required beyond the third day. Intercourse at any time of the day or night carries no possibility of a pregnancy.

DURING MENSTRUAL BLEEDING   Couples should defer intercourse during these days. This ensures that ovulatory signs are not obscured by the bleeding. During a short cycle, ovulation may occur before the bleeding has stopped; and the advice to avoid intercourse at this time takes account of this.

DURING ANY DAY OF BLEEDING BEFORE THE MENSTRUAL PERIOD Avoid intercourse then, and for three days after the appearance of any spots of blood. Such bleeding may coincide with ovulation, and tinge the slippery stretchy mucus pink, brown, red, or yellow. Correct mucus identification is difficult if the bleeding is heavy.

STRESS SITUATIONS   Anxiety, stress, travel, illness or a change of environment may delay ovulation in a cycle even after the chain of events leading to the release of the egg is in motion. If you experience severe stress, for example, you should anticipate the possibility of delayed ovulation, and take special care in evaluating the Peak of fertility. Delaying intercourse in the event of a confused pattern due to stress is a sensible approach.

'My reason for using the method is that I definitely do not want any more children at the present time. I find my capacity to look after my loved three children already strained to the utmost.

I feel that if anyone wants to use the method for this reason, they really need to go into it very thoroughly, and not cut any corners or take risks with it.

At first my husband and I found it very limiting, and certainly not all sweetness and light. Not being able to have intercourse at certain times is a situation that needs to be fully shared and accepted by both partners. As time went on, however, we found this aspect less frustrating; we found we were becoming more aware of each other's needs and feelings. I feel that for us, it has caused a development in our relationship and a deepening of our love.

I would also like to make the point that before I began using the method, I had been on the Pill for twelve months. I did not like being on the Pill at all, and really felt more like a 'thing' than a person. I did not like using chemicals which I knew could have side-effects—and far prefer to know at what stage of the normal cycle I am.'

Guidelines to achieve a pregnancy

Aim to have intercourse two or three times a week before the fertile signs appear, while maintaining a close check on your mucus pattern so that you can detect signs of fertility.

If you usually have several days of fertile mucus in a cycle, aim to have intercourse on these days, as close to the Peak as possible.

If you produce mucus with fertile characteristics only in some cycles, and for only a short time during the cycle, have intercourse at this time. Precision is extremely important for conception. Mucus present for only part of a day is, in some women, sufficient for conception to occur.

CHAPTER 7

Questions often asked

Is the Billings Ovulation Method more suitable for some couples than others?

Yes, most couples in a stable relationship usually find it easier to accept a method that requires some days without intercourse.

The method requires commitment. It appeals most strongly to couples who are motivated to use a natural method and who are willing to take joint responsibility for fertility control. It stabilises and harmonises the relationship.

When the woman knows the days when she will not conceive, she loses her fear and expresses her love generously. Thus mutual love is generated.

How do I know when I am fertile?

Your cervical mucus will indicate your fertility by its characteristics and patterns:
- Following menstruation, a sensation of dryness, with no mucus, indicates infertility.
- Mucus which is flaky, opaque, sticky and scant, and which continues without change day after day also indicates infertility.

- Mucus which differs from either of these patterns suggests an altered level of fertility. If the mucus feels slippery and wet, looks like raw egg-white and can be stretched to form a delicate thread before breaking, you are probably at your most fertile time.

Keeping a daily record will show how the mucus changes from time to time. *The pattern of behaviour of a discharge* is the best way to recognise both fertility and infertility rather than an initial judgement about any particular sample. Every woman's pattern is a little different, but she quickly learns to recognise it herself.

How do I find the mucus?

You will find the mucus at your vaginal opening. You do not need to feel inside the vagina; this will merely confuse the picture because the vagina is always moist. Check for the mucus routinely during the course of the day. Be alert to the sensation it produces, as well as to its appearance. Tuning in to your fertility will soon become second nature to you.

Do I need to keep a chart of my mucus pattern?

Most women find that some sort of recording is necessary as they learn to recognise the different types of discharge associated with fertility and infertility. Don't rely on your memory.

A chart can prove helpful to your partner in giving him an understanding of the changes and communicating your state of fertility. For the purposes of learning, it is advisable to keep a chart for a few months.

Once you are confident that you can recognise your mucus pattern, you can continue with the chart or merely turn your attention to the sensation and appearance of your mucus when you want to know your state of fertility. It is advisable to continue charting if you have a serious reason to avoid pregnancy; or while in a situation of altered fertility such as when approaching the menopause; or, on the other hand, when you want to have a child.

While learning the method should I keep a record of my mucus for a menstrual cycle or for a calendar month?

It is necessary to chart your mucus for two to four weeks only. (If ovulation is delayed for a long time in a cycle, the complete cycle may take several months; charting for this length of time would involve much unnecessary abstinence.) One month is sufficient time for you to assess your state of fertility or infertility.

How many days during a menstrual cycle is the average couple fertile?

Three to six days. Scientific studies show that the egg lives for about twelve hours, and sperm can maintain their fertilising capacity for three to five days if supported by the fertile-type mucus from the cervix. Therefore intercourse on the Peak day or within three to five days beforehand, and before the egg dies after the Peak, may result in a pregnancy.

How many days are available for intercourse in a typical twenty-eight-day cycle? Does this vary according to the length of the cycle or the circumstances of reproductive life—for example, during breastfeeding, or when approaching the menopause?

Results from a World Health Organisation trial of the method indicate that about half the days of a twenty-eight-day cycle are generally available for intercourse. Days of abstinence include the menstrual period, the time when mucus indicates possible fertility, and a safety margin of days to cover individual fertility situations. The rules mean what they say: any relaxation carries the possibility of conception.

In short cycles, fewer than half the days may be available for intercourse, whilst in long cycles, such as when you are breastfeeding or approaching the menopause, considerably more days are available.

Groups of days of abstinence alternate with groups of days available for intercourse, so that abstinence is not required for lengthy periods in any cycle. This is a decided advantage over other natural methods, and an important psychological help in enabling couples to keep to the guidelines.

When intercourse is inadvisable, don't give up loving altogether. There are many ways to show your love, and with imagination these days can be as invigorating and fulfilling as the others.

It is often found helpful to think positively about the phases of the cycle: the fertile phase, with its potential for conceiving a baby, or a time to be set aside by mutual decision; and then the infertile phase, in which you can enjoy totally relaxed sexual loving, free from contraceptive drugs or devices, and fully appreciating each other's expressions of love and concern.

Many couples find that their sexual relationship is revitalised after a short break from intercourse.

You say that sperm can live for up to five days. What if I don't have five days of fertile mucus to warn me that ovulation is approaching?

Sperm cannot pass through the cervix or maintain their fertilising capacity without the presence of fertile mucus because the vaginal environment is hostile to them.

So, if you have fertile mucus for only two days, or even half a day of the cycle, sperm vitality will be reduced correspondingly. The important thing to remember is that when you see or feel the stringy, lubricative mucus you should avoid intercourse then, and for three days afterwards. However many days you see or feel the fertile mucus, you will always have sufficient warning of the approach of ovulation by a change from your infertile pattern.

Why is it important to make love only at night in the first part of the cycle before the fertile mucus becomes apparent?

You need to be on your feet for a few hours so that the fertile mucus can make itself felt or seen. Intercourse upon waking in the morning would not enable you to be aware of a night-time change to fertile mucus and so a pregnancy might result. Once ovulation has occurred and a gap of three days set aside, day or night is available for intercourse.

Why do you advise waiting as soon as there is a change from the infertile pattern?

It is impossible to predict in any cycle just when ovulation will occur. In a short cycle of say twenty-one days, this may happen on about day seven.

The fertile mucus enables sperm to enter the uterus and maintains sperm vitality for up to five days. Without the mucus, sperm fertilising capacity diminishes rapidly. The rule to avoid intercourse when fertile signs become apparent ensures that sperm cells will not retain their fertilising capacity until ovulation.

Fertile signs may begin more than five days before the Peak (the average is six days beforehand). Since it will not be known in any cycle how soon ovulation will occur, the rule to defer intercourse from the first point of change may add a day or two of abstinence which, in retrospect, can be seen to have been unnecessary.

In some cycles, mucus may not appear until very close to ovulation. The same rules will apply, because *sperm transport is blocked and vitality declines quickly without the mucus with fertile characteristics.* The only difference is that during such cycles with a small number of fertile days the time of abstinence will be shorter.

You suggest three days of abstinence after the Peak or last day of fertile mucus. But doesn't the egg die within twelve hours of its release? Thus isn't it impossible to conceive so long after ovulation?

Studies show that the Peak, as identified by a woman herself, correlates closely with ovulation. In about 85 per cent of women it occurs within a day of ovulation and in about 95 per cent within two days (see p. 210).

After the Peak your fertility declines rapidly. A gap of three days after the Peak allows sufficient time for your fertility to decline to zero; within this three days the egg dies, and the cervix is gradually closed by the thick mucus that prevents further sperm entry. By the end of the third day this closure is complete.

How much need my partner know about the method? Should I tell him when I notice the mucus with fertile characteristics so that he knows we cannot make love?

This is one advantage of a chart. Together you can watch your mucus pattern emerge. When your partner understands what it means, he will know the best times for intercourse.

Both partners may feel at times that they would like to throw caution to the wind, even though the mucus indicates fertility. If a couple has decided in advance that this is not the right time for a child, they can support and encourage each other to follow the guidelines. Successful users of the Billings Method have devised many different and individual ways to indicate that it is the fertile phase—a rose in a vase, a chart in an accessible place, or a word about the presence of the characteristic mucus. Many partners experienced in using the method 'just know'.

This shared approach is extremely important. Couples will cope with abstinence, but not with confusion.

Can the guidelines be used more flexibly once a woman has long experience of assessing her own pattern of fertility?

Many women find after using the method for some time that they can enjoy more freedom for intercourse than the guidelines recommend and still avoid pregnancy.

The guidelines have been laid down for maximum security and contain a built-in safety margin. However, couples who adopt a more flexible approach should be prepared for the possibility of a pregnancy.

Can I learn the method with confidence from this book? How important is it to check my mucus observations with a teacher?

Many women will be able to learn the method from this book. However some may find it helpful to consult a trained Billings Method teacher, especially if their pattern is difficult to interpret as may be the case after coming off the Pill or when approaching the menopause.

With whom can I check my chart so that I know I am interpreting my mucus signals correctly?

The best person to advise you about your chart is a trained teacher of the Billings Method. Details of a centre near you can be obtained from the Billings Family Life Centre, 27 Alexandra Parade, North Fitzroy, Victoria 3068, Australia; *email* billings@ozemail.com.au

Doesn't this method take the spontaneity out of love-making?

The use of any natural method means that you can't always have intercourse when you feel like it. To avoid a pregnancy, you can't have intercourse when you are fertile. This approach needs to be discussed and mutually agreed upon by partners when they decide to use the method.

Weighed against this are the many days when love-making can be completely spontaneous, free from drugs and devices, and from any doubts about your state of fertility.

What relationship does the mucus with fertile characteristics have to ovulation?

From an average of six days before ovulation, mucus begins which soon takes on lubricative, stringy qualities and looks like raw egg-white.

This characteristic mucus is caused by rising levels of the hormone oestrogen acting on the cervix. All the evidence suggests that it is essential for movement of sperm and maintenance of their fertilising capacity, and is therefore a reliable warning signal that you are fertile.

The Peak of fertility—which corresponds closely with ovulation—is the last day of any sensation or appearance of the mucus with fertile characteristics. *It is not the day of maximum mucus. This is a common error.* (The sensation of lubrication may continue for a day or two after visible mucus disappears—but the continuation of the sensation and of vulval swelling indicate that you are still fertile.)

How do you account for the changes in the cervical mucus?

A number of studies have investigated the changing nature of the mucus and have linked these changes with hormones. Basically, the different types of mucus are produced in response to different levels of the hormones oestrogen and progesterone. These hormones come from the ovary. They act directly on the cervix to stimulate the formation of the different types of mucus that you will see and feel. The fertile mucus becomes apparent as the egg begins to mature in response to a rising oestrogen level. Following ovulation, progesterone causes the cervix to produce the sticky, dense mucus, and a dramatic change in sensation. Photographs on p. 136 show the different appearances of the mucus.

I can recognise changes in the appearance of my mucus, but I am not confident of my ability to detect changes in sensation. Does this mean I should not use this method?

No. Whilst both the sensation and appearance of the mucus are important indicators of your state of fertility, awareness and recognition of these may take time to develop. Persevere with the method, and take the time to chart your mucus pattern. Many women find that their ability to detect sensations develops rapidly and becomes second nature to them. Studies show that most women can produce a recognisable mucus pattern after only one month of learning the method.

Is the mucus with fertile characteristics always clear?

No, this mucus may be cloudy, or it may be tinged red, pink, or brown, from blood, a few drops of which may be produced just before ovulation.

Although the appearance of this mucus varies, its consistency resembles raw egg-white, and it always has the characteristic of slipperiness or lubricativeness. Occasionally, some women see no mucus but feel the lubricating sensation, *indicating that they are fertile.*

Is it always easy to see the mucus?

Most women see, as well as feel, the different types of mucus during their cycles. A very few women say they see very little, if any, mucus but are aware of an unmistakable sensation for which even small amounts of mucus are responsible.

Does stress affect the mucus pattern?

Stress due to emotional upset or illness may delay ovulation and lengthen cycles. Regular strenuous exertion may eliminate ovulation and menstruation. There is no evidence to indicate that stress speeds up ovulation.

Is it possible to conceive without producing the characteristic mucus?

All the evidence suggests that mucus with fertile characteristics must be produced by the cervix for conception to occur (see chapter 15). This is because the mucus assists sperm transport and provides the environment in the vagina that is necessary for the maintenance of sperm fertilising capacity. On the basis of this evidence considerable doubt must be expressed about the possibility of a pregnancy when mucus is not produced.

The importance of this mucus is now recognised by infertility workers throughout the world. Couples having difficulty conceiving are advised to be alert for mucus with fertile characteristics and to use these days for intercourse.

Any delay in ovulation will be mirrored by your mucus. For example, if severe stress occurs in the few days preceding ovulation, you will notice that the characteristic mucus suddenly stops and is replaced either by a BIP of discharge or by dryness.

Because it may be difficult to be sure at such a time whether ovulation has occurred, a gap of three days should be allowed before resuming intercourse on alternate evenings, and the Early Day Rules (p. 47) be continued until the Peak is recognised. Remember that intercourse is confined to evenings at this stage of your cycle to allow confirmation of the Basic Infertile Pattern during the day. Occasionally severe stress may result in a confused pattern of mucus and it is advisable to postpone intercourse during this time.

Can intercourse trigger ovulation?

Hormonal studies on humans have not been able to establish a relationship between intercourse and ovulation.

If couples don't wish to conceive, intercourse should be deferred as soon as signs of fertility become apparent, and for three days past the Peak.

Can knowledge of my mucus pattern help me identify infection or disease?

Yes, women who get to know their normal body processes may often be aware immediately anything goes wrong.

If the mucus pattern changes significantly—for example, there may be a sudden increase in the amount of mucus, or the colour or odour of the mucus may alter—it is a good idea to consult a doctor. An altered pattern may be due to disorders such as polycystic ovaries (see p. 153) or infection.

Gynaecologists are paying increasing attention to these changes, for they may indicate an abnormality or disease of the reproductive organs, a hormonal upset or a side-effect of medication. The earlier a disorder is diagnosed—for example, cancer of the cervix—the greater the probability of a successful treatment.

Do any drugs affect the mucus?

Yes, indirectly, the following drugs alter the mucus pattern, with variable effects in different women:
• Some tranquillisers, e.g. Largactil, by causing raised prolactin resulting in delayed ovulation. (However,

when ovulation does occur, it will be recognised by the familiar mucus pattern.)

- Hormones, for example, progesterone and oestrogens.
- Antihistamines (some women only are affected; individual charting will soon determine this).
- Cytotoxic drugs used in the treatment of cancer. These prevent mucus production by a direct action on the ovaries.
- Antibiotics. Women taking antibiotics for a severe illness sometimes notice a change in the mucus pattern. This is an effect induced by the stress of the illness and not the drug. Women on continuous antibiotics for chronic illness can interpret their mucus pattern successfully.

Do vaginal sprays and douches alter the mucus pattern?

Yes. They produce an artificial wetness which may confuse your interpretations of the mucus. They may also cause an allergic reaction or inflammation, resulting in an infective discharge which alters the mucus pattern.

While cleanliness is essential to good health and an important consideration in a sexual relationship, it is unnecessary and inadvisable to use these preparations to clean the vagina. The vagina is self-cleansing, and external washing is quite adequate.

What changes to the mucus can I expect after a curettage? Can I still use the Billings Method effectively?

The stress of a curettage may delay ovulation and therefore postpone the production of the mucus with fertile signs.

It is advisable to avoid intercourse until the Peak is recognised because the mucus pattern may be temporarily disturbed and unfamiliar. Then apply the method guidelines as usual.

Women who have recently had a curettage may not feel well enough to enjoy intercourse. If this disinclination is discussed with your partner ahead of time, it can be accepted with understanding.

Is there any reason why my partner and I should not use withdrawal during my fertile time?

Withdrawal is not a good idea for two reasons.

Firstly, your partner may lose a drop of semen before orgasm, and this usually contains sperm, which could lead to an unintended pregnancy.

Secondly, withdrawal is often unsatisfactory for both man and woman. Your partner can't relax because he knows that he has to withdraw before ejaculating; and you can't relax because you know he may fail to do so. The anxiety is pointless because it is now established that fertile mucus outside the vagina enables sperm cells to find their way to the Fallopian tubes and the awaiting egg cell. Penetration is not necessary for conception.

Also, withdrawal usually occurs before a woman reaches, or completes, an orgasm. This can lead to considerable mutual frustration and discontent.

Clinical reports indicate that withdrawal may be responsible for sexual passivity in women who would rather suppress their responses than endure frequently repeated frustration when intercourse stops short of orgasm.

Can I combine physical methods of contraception, such as the condom and diaphragm, with the Billings Method?

No. There is a good biological reason for not using barrier methods during your fertile phase. The seminal fluid and vaginal secretions associated with intercourse will tend to confuse your mucus pattern and will make it much more difficult to assess your state of fertility correctly. There is no surer way to avoid a pregnancy than avoidance of intercourse when you are fertile. In addition, all the barrier contraceptives have a method failure rate and using a condom or a diaphragm at the fertile time may result in a pregnancy.

I seem to have only a trace of mucus. Is the amount of mucus produced important?

For conception to occur, it is essential that some mucus is produced, because without it, sperm cannot survive to reach and fertilise the egg. However, often women think they have little or no mucus until they start to keep a daily record. They then become alert to the mucus, and realise that they are producing much more than they had thought.

If, after charting, you find that you are producing only a little mucus, this may be quite normal. Your Basic Infertile Pattern may be one of dryness, and when your level of fertility changes, you will notice a small amount of mucus with fertile characteristics. The sensation will change.

If you are completely dry throughout the cycle, your fertility may be impaired and it is wise to consult a doctor.

I feel a lot of wetness before making love when I've been dry all day. Is this fertile mucus?

It may be fertile mucus that has just begun to be produced by the cervix. But it may be the lubricating mucus produced by the vagina in response to sexual excitement.

If you check your mucus during the day and in the evening, before you are even thinking about making love, you will gain a clear indication of your state of fertility.

The fertile days are usually heralded by a sticky, cloudy mucus after dry days. Or you may notice a plug of mucus. This pattern changes to a stretchy, lubricative mucus nearer to the Peak. Charting will reveal your individual pattern. You will soon be able to recognise the effect of sexual intercourse on your mucus pattern. A chart which shows the effect of intercourse on the mucus pattern is illustrated on p. 131.

I feel more sexually interested when my mucus is of the fertile type. Is there a biological explanation for this?

Yes. The mucus is exceptionally lubricative at the time of ovulation, and is therefore ideal for intercourse. This may be the reason for your heightened libido at this time. Other factors which some couples notice are an arousing odour associated with the fertile-type mucus, and a fullness of the tissues around the vagina. These characteristics are due to a high level of oestrogen hormone produced by the ovaries when you are fertile.

After the fertile phase, I sometimes feel uninterested in sexual intercourse. Why is this? Can it be overcome?

The basic reason for this disinclination is hormonal. After ovulation the level of oestrogen hormone declines. This is associated with a decline in the lubricative mucus produced by the cervix, which assists intercourse. Its place is taken by a drier thicker mucus produced by the cervix under the influence of progesterone. The resulting dryness can be overcome by an unhurried preparation for love-making which allows secretions to develop in the glands around the vaginal opening and allows the vulva to become lubricated.

The level of progesterone hormone increases after ovulation. This is associated with an emotional let-down. 'I couldn't when I wanted to, so now I don't want to' is a frequent initial reaction. You may find that you need to make a conscious effort to be affectionate. This ability is something that grows and a man needs to understand this and encourage its development by special attention at this time.

Hormonal changes during the cycle are only one factor in a woman's feeling of emotional well-being and enjoyment of intercourse. Love-making in the infertile part of the cycle can be very satisfying because it is based on loving consideration by both partners.

Will I become pregnant if I make love on the first day after noticing a change from my Basic Infertile Pattern?

The change from an infertile pattern indicates an alteration in hormone levels and therefore possible fertility. You thus increase your chances of becoming pregnant if you make love on that day.

Some couples experiment with these early days of fertile mucus, and find that they do not conceive. But if couples are strongly motivated to avoid a pregnancy, they should avoid intercourse on any day when the mucus indicates possible fertility, because sooner or later deviation from the guidelines may result in conception. This may come as a surprise to couples who have consistently found such a day infertile.

A friend of mine says she conceived after making love during her period. Is this possible?

It is possible to conceive during your period, particularly if your cycles are very short. The shorter your cycle, the earlier you ovulate, because you ovulate about two weeks before your following menstrual period. For example, if you make love on the sixth day of bleeding and ovulate on day nine of a twenty-four-day cycle, you could become pregnant.

Your mucus will warn you of your increasing fertility by becoming stringy and lubricative. However, since it may be obscured by your menstrual bleeding, it is advisable

SIMPLE WAYS OF EXPLAINING THE METHOD

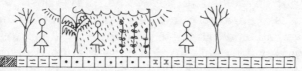

BLEED	DRY	MUCUS	1 2 3

Flower seed in dry soil — Rain comes flower grows — Rain stopped soil still wet — Flower dies

An illustration used to explain the method to Aboriginal women in Darwin, Australia

Teaching the method to village women in Ruanda, Africa

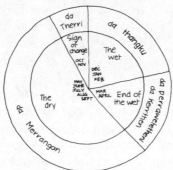

Dry ground infertile — Rain grass grows fertile — Dry ground infertile

Teaching the method in El Salvador, central America

A chart from an Aboriginal mission near Darwin, relating the seasons to a woman's cycle

to avoid intercourse while you are menstruating.

It is also worth remembering that the spots of blood that may immediately precede ovulation later in the cycle are sometimes confused with another menstruation. Intercourse at such a time is highly likely to result in conception.

Most books say menstruation happens fourteen days after ovulation, yet you quote a range of eleven to sixteen days. Don't most women experience a fourteen-day post-ovulatory phase?

About half of all fertile women have post-ovulatory phases of thirteen or fourteen days most of the time. The other half tend to have ten to twelve, or fifteen to sixteen, days between ovulation and menstruation. An individual woman tends to keep the same interval of time between ovulation and menstruation.

I have been using the Pill for the past three years. Can I switch to this method immediately?

Yes. The first step is to stop taking the Pill. Then, start to chart your pattern of discharges. After about a month's charting you should be able to recognise if you are fertile or infertile. During this month it is advisable to avoid intercourse, so that your pattern is not obscured by seminal fluid or vaginal secretions associated with intercourse. After this time you will be able to use the method guidelines.

Many women are infertile for some months after coming off the Pill, and the mucus pattern will have infertile characteristics which you will soon come to recognise. Any change from this pattern suggests altered fertility, and the need for a brief period without intercourse as your fertility returns. Coming off the Pill is discussed in chapter 9. A chart of a woman who discontinued the Pill is shown on p. 132.

When coming off the Pill, should I wait for my first period before beginning to chart my mucus pattern?

No, it is not necessary to wait for your first period—this may not occur for several months. As soon as you stop taking the Pill, start charting within two to four weeks. You will be able to recognise from your mucus whether you are fertile or infertile, and to apply the guidelines reliably.

I am twenty-three and my cycles are long and irregular. Do I need hormone treatment to reduce them to the average length in order to use the Billings Method?

Irregularity of cycles is no obstacle to using the method. This is because you assess your mucus signals of fertility and infertility on a day-to-day basis rather than relying on a rigid calendar rule.

There is no need to alter the length of your cycles. Hormone treatment for this purpose is now discouraged by leading medical authorities because it disrupts normal physical and emotional patterns. In some cases, the disturbance caused by hormone treatment may be so great as to result in prolonged infertility. This is due to damage to the cervix. If the mechanisms of ovulation are damaged, this may be demonstrated by a short interval between ovulation and menstruation, following the Peak. It takes time for nature to restore normality; hormone treatment should be avoided.

A possible cause of very irregular cycles is that you are not ovulating. This may be due to a number of factors (see p. 151). If charting your mucus indicates that you are not ovulating, further medical investigation is necessary.

Is it necessary to maintain abstinence during menstrual bleeding if your body, over a long period, does not have short cycles?

There is no guarantee that your body will always follow the same pattern. Often the onset of the pre-menopause is marked by a very short cycle in which ovulation occurs during the menstrual bleeding. Therefore if you have intercourse during menstruation, you leave yourself open to the possibility of a pregnancy.

My cycles average only twenty-one days. Then, very soon after the days of menstrual bleeding, I notice slippery mucus. Can I use the Billings Method?

Yes, the length of cycle does not alter the applicability of the method.

Your early ovulation, as indicated by the mucus with fertile characteristics, means that you will have few, if any, early infertile days. But intercourse can be resumed from three days after your Peak of fertility and, of course, if cycles are short, your post-ovulatory infertility, which is free of all restrictions, returns more frequently.

I have been trying to have a baby for more than a year, but without success. Can I use the Billings Method to become pregnant?

To increase your chances of having a baby to the maximum, you will need to follow the method guidelines in reverse. Once you have read this book carefully and understand the principles of fertility, start to chart your mucus to find out if and when you are ovulating. The mucus with fertile characteristics will indicate your fertile phase. It may not occur in every cycle. The fertile mucus may last for several days or only half a day in a cycle, so you may need to watch carefully for it. Aim to have intercourse every few days whilst keeping a close check on your mucus, and when the fertile mucus becomes apparent, use these days. When the mucus is stringy like raw egg-white, and lubricative, the sperm cells will have the best chance of fertilising the egg.

Fertility clinics the world over now recognise the importance of the cervical mucus. For example, doctors involved in artificial insemination realise that it is useless to inseminate a woman except when she is producing mucus with fertile characteristics.

Can the Billings Method be used to influence the sex of a baby?

The scientific evidence on this is controversial.

Some users say that making love early in the development of the characteristic mucus—with no other intercourse during that cycle—tends to result in a girl; while intercourse confined to the day of Peak fertility tends to result in a boy.

A study in Nigeria appeared to confirm this tendency. This study was based on the theory that a single act of intercourse at the Peak would result in a boy; while intercourse when the mucus changed from sticky and became slippery before the Peak, with no further intercourse until after the fertile phase was over, would result in a girl.

According to the study co-ordinator, Dr (Sr) Leonie McSweeney:[1]

Success in pre-selection of a boy was achieved by 310 couples. Failure in pre-selection of a boy occurred in four couples. Success in pre-selection of a girl was achieved in 90 couples. Failure in pre-selection of a girl occurred in two couples.

Others who have tried to use the method to pre-select the sex of a child have generally achieved a lower success rate. Pre-determination of the sex of a baby is never likely to be 100 per cent reliable.

Will hormone or other treatments enable a woman to produce the fertile mucus and thus help her to conceive?

Judicious use of gonadotrophins may enhance ovulation, thereby improving the mucus quality and achieving a successful pregnancy.

What is the reason for a statistically low pregnancy rate in rape?

Statistically, the chances of rape coinciding with ovulation or the mucus with fertile characteristics are slight. (The chances of pregnancy from rape in the United States has been estimated at one per thousand cases.) It may be that the severe stress of such an attack would delay the ovulation process; so that the sperm cells die before the egg leaves the ovary. It is often thought that curettage removes the sperm cells, but this is not so. The curettage removes the uterine lining, so that if a fertilised egg does eventuate, there is nowhere for it to implant.

The 'morning-after' pill disrupts the cycle. Given up to half a day before ovulation, it will prevent conception by delaying ovulation. Very specific hormonal information is required, but seldom available, in order to determine the imminence of ovulation. Given after conception it will cause abortion by preventing implantation of the embryo, and this is its usual effect. It is important for every woman to know the fertile signs, so that in the event of rape she can assess the possibility of conception at once.

Sometimes I see a small blood loss about two weeks before my period. What does this mean?

Such 'spotting' may indicate ovulation. It is due to a high level of the hormone oestrogen acting on the endometrium or lining of the uterus, and causing a seepage of blood through it, a day or two before ovulation.

The blood loss is usually slight and gives the mucus a tinge of colour. Occasionally it is quite heavy, particularly during a long cycle, and it may obscure the mucus. Hence the importance of the guideline to defer intercourse on any day of bleeding, and for three days afterwards.

Although the blood loss usually occurs close to ovulation, it is not experienced by a great percentage of women, and is therefore not a reliable guide to ovulation.

I have a chronic discharge due to cysts of the cervix. Can I use the Billings Method?

Yes. By charting your mucus daily, you will soon learn to recognise the pattern of mucus associated with a chronic condition. Even when a chronic discharge exists, a change will be noticed in the pattern when the state of fertility alters.

The discharge accompanying cervical cysts is variable and may be a continuous, wet, slippery mucus. The abnormality should be rectified, resulting in the return of your normal pattern.

In the case of an acute infection, such as that caused by the fungus *Candida albicans* (monilia), also known as 'thrush', your mucus pattern will be altered, as it may be by T-mycoplasma, gonorrhoea or trichomonas. These require treatment, during which it is advisable not to have intercourse. This is because intercourse may break up the colonies or organisms and cause them to spread, for example, to the urinary system or to your partner. Local agents used for treating thrush tend to cause drying out of the discharge and the mucus. Therefore wait until after treatment and the return of your normal mucus pattern before resuming intercourse.

Is it possible to ovulate twice in a cycle? Does this affect the reliability of the guidelines?

It is possible to release two or more eggs in a cycle but studies show this always occurs *on the same day.* So all aspects of the Billings Method still apply: the guidelines are not affected by multiple ovulation.

During my cycle I sometimes experience pain in the lower abdomen or back, which can be quite sharp. Is this a sign of ovulation?

Some women commonly experience such a pain during their cycles. Studies show that this may be related to the overall rise in hormones associated with ovulation. The pain may be sharp, or dull, rather like a period pain.

The mechanism of this pain production is not fully understood. In many cases it occurs when the oestrogens rise even when ovulation does not occur. It may be due to contractions of muscle tissue in the uterus in response to hormones; or the pain may be due to muscle-sensitising chemicals (prostaglandins) found in seminal fluid which set off a hormonal response, said to affect the activity of muscles in the female reproductive organs.

Since the pain does not always coincide with ovulation, it is not a reliable guide to fertility.

How accurate is a temperature rise in indicating ovulation? Does keeping a temperature chart help in the recognition of the fertile phase? Is there a place for temperature measurements in natural birth control?

Temperature is not a completely reliable or accurate indicator of ovulation. Studies show that a rise in temperature may occur up to four days before, to six days after, ovulation,[2] although in some cycles it occurs on the day of ovulation. A false high temperature may be caused by a fever. If you rely on this reading for proof of ovulation, you could become pregnant. And in some fertile cycles, no temperature rise occurs around the time of ovulation.

Temperature readings have no value in *predicting* when you will ovulate—a necessity in any effective natural fertility control method.

Another disadvantage is that if you defer intercourse until you see a temperature rise, and if this does not occur until late in your cycle, the time available for love-making is greatly and unnecessarily restricted. In addition, you are advised to take your temperature for some minutes every morning after at least three hours sleep, and before getting out of bed, eating or drinking. This can become tiresome and a source of irritation, and in the case of a mother who is disturbed at night by waking children, it may be impossible.

Even when temperature readings are combined with mucus awareness, the result is not always satisfactory. For a temperature rise may not occur until several days after you see or feel fertile mucus. Thus temperature recordings may cause confusion, and can divert attention from the mucus, which is the more accurate guide to your state of fertility.

Under normal circumstances the routine taking of temperature is unwarranted. However, temperature measurements may prove of value when no recognisable mucus pattern is apparent (for example, due to a defective cervix), or when the mucus is temporarily obscured by an erratic discharge, provided ovulation is occurring.

Where a woman is trying to conceive and is recording a poor mucus pattern, a rise in her basal body temperature will indicate that she is ovulating and that further investigation is necessary.

Might I ovulate but not produce any mucus with fertile characteristics?

Yes, this is possible. The cycle will then be infertile, because the sperm fertilising capacity diminishes rapidly without the fertile mucus. Clinical investigations show that this situation occurs in some women who have difficulty conceiving. The problem is the subject of intensive research: some causes have been found, leading to successful treatment and pregnancy.

It is not uncommon for young women to experience an occasional ovulatory cycle without mucus. And the occurrence of such infertile cycles becomes common in women nearing the menopause, when the cervix becomes unresponsive to rising hormones; this, in part, accounts for declining fertility. The Pill is often responsible for a poor cervical response even when you are ovulating normally. Patience and nature are the best healers.

I find intercourse painful and uncomfortable and have been using lubricants to help overcome this problem. Since I wish to have a baby, is this advisable?

The problem of a dry vagina can be overcome by unhurried and loving preparation for intercourse, which allows the vagina to produce its own lubricating secretions.

Artificial lubricants often contain chemicals that kill sperm or make the environment of the vagina hostile to them. So it is best to avoid their use if you want a baby. Lubricants also tend to obscure the fertile mucus by their artificial wetness, so making it difficult to time intercourse to coincide with your Peak of fertility. The sensation of slipperiness is the best indicator of fertility and usually persists for a day or two after the strings have disappeared. The last day of slipperiness is the Peak.

I have had three children in close succession and have not experienced a period during this time. Can the Billings Method help me know when my fertility returns after the birth of a child?

Yes; the awareness of your mucus will enable you to recognise when your fertility returns after childbirth. And by following the Billings Method guidelines you will be able to space your children as you wish.

The births of your three children close together indicate that you conceived each time during your first fertile cycle after childbirth.

I am breastfeeding and have no periods yet; so I am relying on my mucus changes to warn me of my first ovulation. However, I seem to be producing wet mucus all the time. Does this mean I am fertile now?

If your mucus is continually wet, and has remained the same for two weeks or more without bleeding, this is your Basic Infertile Pattern and indicates infertility.

As soon as there is any *change* from this constant situation you will know that your hormone levels are rising. Oestrogens often fluctuate for a month or two before your first ovulation and period. The return of fertility depends to a large extent on the age and sucking habits of your baby.

If you wish to avoid a pregnancy, apply the Early Day Rules. If your mucus pattern changes frequently causing confusion, postpone intercourse until the fourth day after you have recognised the Peak. A trained Billings Method teacher is the best person to guide you through this time of hormone adjustment.

When preparing for a successful and enjoyable breastfeeding experience with your baby, it is most important that you understand the associated infertility of this period: that it is a time during which you and your partner are free to have intercourse with security. If a temporary period without intercourse is necessary as your fertility returns, frustration can be avoided by couples discussing this possibility ahead of time.

I noticed that when my menstrual periods began after the birth of my daughter, they started about one week after ovulation, as indicated by both the mucus fertile characteristics and the Peak. Would this be a fertile cycle?

The cycle is not a fertile one if menstruation starts less than eleven days after ovulation.

This situation is common during and after breastfeeding

and is due to the effects of the 'milk hormone' prolactin. A shortened interval between ovulation and menstruation can also occur as you approach the menopause, or after stopping the Pill.

My periods come only every few months now as I am forty-three. What should I do about avoiding pregnancy?

If you don't have a period very often, then you are not ovulating very often either, if at all. You can rely on the mucus from the cervix to inform you of possible fertility. By being alert to mucus changes and by following the guidelines, you can avoid a pregnancy.

After reading this book, chart your mucus for a month, whilst avoiding intercourse to ensure a clear picture of your mucus pattern. Typically, the pattern is one of long phases of infertility interspersed by occasional episodes of possible fertility. *The recognition of infertility is of paramount importance.*

A trained Billings Ovulation Method teacher will help guide you through this phase of your reproductive life if you are having difficulties. She will be able to provide the information to overcome any problems; solutions are usually not difficult.

I am forty-six, and my cycles are very irregular. I am worried about becoming pregnant, but my doctor advised against the Pill because I suffer from high blood pressure. Would I be able to use the Billings Method?

Yes; the Billings Method is particularly helpful in situations such as yours. Past the age of forty, fertility diminishes substantially, and cycles become irregular as hormones fluctuate.

By charting your mucus you may find that even though your periods continue, you are infertile most of the time. Ovulation without mucus is infertile.

So you need to be able to *recognise infertility.* This positive recognition of infertility is a feature of the Billings Method not shared by other natural methods such as the Rhythm and Temperature methods.

After charting for a month or so, you will be able to recognise when you are infertile. Any change in the mucus suggests possible fertility. There is no need to be concerned about whether you have reached the menopause. All you need to recognise are the changes in your infertile pattern. Occasionally days of mucus will remind you that your fertility is still fluctuating.

Recent trials of the Billings Method indicate a 'method effectiveness' of better than 99 per cent. What does this mean?

These figures are based on a number of trials throughout the world which indicated that if 100 couples use the method according to the guidelines for avoiding pregnancy, one pregnancy or none at all will occur. We don't know why this is so. Sometimes information is withheld until later. No method can claim 100 per cent effectiveness.

This method effectiveness compares extremely well with other methods: the Pill (99 per cent), Mini Pill (96 per cent), IUD (94 to 99 per cent), Rhythm (53 to 86 per cent).

The actual pregnancy rate in some Billings Method trials is about 20 per cent. Why is this?

The vast majority of pregnancies occur when couples knowingly ignore the guidelines. This is often because they are uncertain about the desirability of having children. Other reasons exist which are very complex and personal. Couples are free to use the method as they wish.

A minority of pregnancies result from inadequate teaching, and others when couples misinterpret the mucus. Pregnancies are extremely rare among couples who co-operate with each other, are well informed about the method, and are motivated to make it work.

The term 'continuation rate' is often mentioned when fertility control methods are discussed. What is this?

Statistically it refers to the percentage of women still using a method after a given time. The continuation rate for the Billings Method was 98 per cent after four years in an early Melbourne study of pre-menopausal women.[3] High continuation rates were also recorded in later trials, in the USA,[4] Indonesia,[5] India,[6] and China.[7] (See chapter 16.)

Are there any devices available to check whether ovulation is imminent or has occurred?

Professor J.B. Brown of Melbourne University has developed one such device, the Ovarian Meter (see p. 215).

From time to time, devices for detecting ovulation appear on the market, but as yet none is as universally applicable or as accurate as the Ovarian Meter.

CHAPTER 8

Learning about fertility in adolescence

When a girl is born her ovaries each contain half a million or so follicles which are spheres of cells containing all the eggs that will be released during her fertile life. Only 300–500 of these will develop into mature eggs. The other follicles degenerate before completing development, many before puberty.

Each girl has her own 'biological clock', centred in the brain, that sets her menstrual cycles in motion. At puberty, generally between the ages of eleven and fourteen in girls, the pituitary gland just below the brain, influenced by the 'clock', signals the ovaries to begin producing the oestrogen hormones in sufficient amounts to cause breast enlargement, maturing of the sex organs, and emotional changes. Changes in the uterus also occur which make menstruation possible.

The beginning of the bleeding is called the menarche and it usually occurs at about thirteen years of age although it may occur as early as nine or as late as seventeen.

The first year or two is a time of irregular bleeding for most girls, but then the cycle settles down to a pattern (usually of twenty-three to thirty-five days) from the beginning of bleeding to the last day before the next period begins. This phase of fluctuating hormones plays an important role in growth processes and future reproduction. Natural irregularities of cycle length should on no account be manipulated by the Pill and other hormones to bring about regularity. Women can be quite healthy and have irregular cycles all their reproductive lives; no treatment is necessary.

Most girls do not ovulate for the first year or so after bleeding begins, that is, their ovaries do not release an egg ready for fertilisation and a possible pregnancy. The hormones are priming the reproductive system, getting it ready for later fertility.

So in the beginning the signs of fertility may not be present. By knowing about the mucus changes that signal the body's emerging fertility, you can recognise it when it arrives. At first there will be odd episodes of sticky or flaky mucus coming from the vagina. Gradually, over several months, the cyclical fertile pattern of slippery, stringy mucus will be seen. (See chapter 4.)

With ovulation the second hormone from the ovary, progesterone, plays its part, producing a change from the fertile mucus pattern.

Hormones (the Pill) given to eliminate ovulation and stop menstrual pain have serious consequences,[1] which can include future infertility. When these hormones are accompanied by smoking, dangerous effects on blood vessels in the brain, with stroke, have been reported. Other treatments available for pain are not harmful.

It is important to have a clear understanding of the signs of fertility. This knowledge is healthy and useful throughout life. It is also a good feeling to tune into the rhythms of your body. Moreover it is a matter of some convenience to be able to anticipate the menstrual bleedings. It is also important to know that the fertile mucus is not a disease requiring treatment: it is a normal, healthy sign.

The first four chapters of this book explain the menstrual cycle and describe how you can develop an awareness of when you are fertile by understanding the mucus signs. The mucus—as well as providing the sign—plays a vital role in fertility, because it is essential for maintaining the vitality of the sperm cells. Because the fertile mucus is so favourable to sperm cells, they can travel through it into the body, reach the egg, and fertilise it, even if close sexual contact without actual intercourse has occurred. All this can happen when mucus is present on the body outside the vagina.

Don't trust your mucus record to memory. It is vital to keep a chart while you are learning about your fertility. The pictures on p. 136 show what the mucus might look like, but everyone is different. Note feelings of swelling and slipperiness of the vulva, which indicate high fertility.

Remember that ovulation occurs about fourteen days (the range is eleven to sixteen days) before your menstrual period and will be indicated in advance by the mucus. Some women have been led to believe that ovulation always occurs at the mid-point of the cycle. Although this may be true in a twenty-eight-day cycle, it is not so in a short cycle of say eighteen days (when ovulation may occur at about day four, perhaps before your period has finished), or in a long cycle of, for example, thirty-five days (when ovulation will take place on about day twenty-one). Within the same woman, the timing of ovulation can vary significantly from cycle to cycle. Hence it is important that you are able to determine, by observing the mucus, when you ovulate in *each cycle*, rather than depending on ovulation occurring at the same time each month.

Stress resulting from excessive exercise may cause ovulatory delays and irregular bleeding. Moderation in exercise is healthier. Other stresses, for example illness, exams, grief and rape, can delay ovulation. It is not uncommon for a sexually active girl to experience a long cycle in fear that she is pregnant because her expected menstruation does not come. If she knows her signs of fertility and if she has avoided complete genital contact for this time, she will be spared anxiety.

Recently contraceptive under-the-skin implants of etonorgestrel (Implanol), replaced every three years, have been recommended for young athletes. This is a progestogen and operates by suppressing ovulation, causing cervical mucus changes which inhibit sperm migration, and interfering with the uterine lining making it unsuitable for implantation of an embryo should conception occur. The risks, contraindications and damage to fertility are the same as for all chemical contraceptives.

The female reproductive system matures slowly over several years. A young woman should weigh up the health risks of early sexual activity. The risk of cervical cancer is higher among women who start sexual relationships at an early age, and who have more than one sexual partner.[2]

Venereal warts, genital herpes, smoking and the contraceptive pill are all contributory factors in the development of cancer of the cervix. Healthy bone growth is jeopardised by smoking and the Pill, with fragility and possible fractures developing in later life. The use of contraceptive implants and injections carry a high risk to reproductive health (see chapter 13).

Future fertility can be jeopardised by venereal disease, especially gonorrhoea, if it is not diagnosed early.[3] By the time symptoms develop, or even severe illness, the fine lining of the Fallopian tubes may already be damaged, preventing the transport of sperm and egg, or causing the fertilised egg to lodge in the tube instead of the uterus. Damage to tubes from venereal disease, for example chlamydial infection, cannot be undone.

If you are involved in a sexual relationship, the greatest dilemma you could face could arise from pregnancy.

Every act of intercourse in the fertile phase carries with it the possibility of pregnancy. So the possibility of conceiving a baby needs to be carefully considered if the prospect of intercourse arises. Some of the information given to adolescents concentrates on methods of contraception, without mentioning that the best and most foolproof method of avoiding pregnancy is abstinence. It is worth thinking about possible consequences of these problems now. It is apparent that many young women realise their responsibility for their own body and what happens to it. They are entitled to hope to find one day a partner with views and ambitions similar to their own, instead of feeling they must conform to other people's ideas.

If a pregnancy does occur and an abortion is contemplated, it is worth considering that damage to the cervix in order to abort may cause it to become incapable of carrying a later pregnancy to term.

AIDS   AIDS is caused by a virus that is present in all body fluids—in genital secretions, saliva, blood and breast milk. The virus is fragile outside the body and will not live on such things as baths and toilet seats. Infection is caused by direct passage of the virus between individuals: from man to man, from man to woman, woman to man, and by a woman to her baby during pregnancy and breastfeeding.

Sharing syringes used for injecting drugs is particularly dangerous. Anal intercourse is especially conducive to infection. As AIDS can be transmitted heterosexually, having multiple sexual partners increases the risk. The disease has devastated some countries, particularly in Africa and Asia. The virus attacks the immune system by destroying the normally protective white blood cells. Once a patient has been infected, sooner or later various signs of the disease appear and lead inevitably to death. Medications have been developed which are beneficial in prolonging the lives of HIV/AIDS sufferers. The search for a vaccine continues.

It is known that the use of condoms in general reduces the overall spread of sexually transmitted diseases. However, the advocation of condoms by public health authorities has promoted a false sense of security, particularly amongst young people. Condoms, which act by blocking the transmission of sperm cells, can break and spill, and have a considerable failure rate in preventing pregnancy. The HIV virus is much smaller, and its transmission has been reported despite condom use. The only way to be free of the threat of HIV AIDS which is sexually transmitted is to live in a one-to-one relationship with someone who also lives this way.

Conclusion

Adolescence should be a carefree time of bodies developing, minds maturing, friendships being forged, and dreams being dreamed. This chapter may at times have made bleak reading, but it is intended to help you make informed choices on matters which will affect your future happiness and health.

You will find in the back of the book a list of addresses where the Billings Method is taught. Write or email for the address of a teaching centre near you. You will find the guidance of a trained Billings Method teacher helpful in interpreting your mucus pattern. You will enjoy this experience of getting to know yourself and the treasure of your fertility.

CHAPTER 9

Coming off the Pill

Coming off the Pill can stimulate a reassessment of your relationship. Many couples who are postponing or spacing a family, and who are using the Pill as their fertility control method, find themselves in a position where they no longer discuss contraception. There is a tendency to assume that the woman will continue to take responsibility for birth control and to bear its health burden. What may have been intended initially as a temporary contraceptive measure often becomes an ingrained habit, so that decisions about long-term birth control may be deferred indefinitely.

This situation can breed unhappiness and resentment, particularly among women suffering from Pill-induced ill-health. In such a situation, a woman suffering side-effects from the Pill often responds very positively to learning the Billings Method and her partner is very happy to have her in good health and spirits again.

If a man acknowledges that part of the responsibility for fertility control rests with him, he is usually willing to accept the co-operation and days without intercourse necessary for successful use of the method.

The first step

If you have decided to use the Billings Method, the first step is to discontinue the Pill. You don't have to wait until you finish your present course of tablets . . . the sooner you stop taking the Pill, the sooner you can begin to chart your mucus pattern. It is no use trying to learn the method while still taking the Pill; for the synthetic hormones of the Pill alter the mucus pattern.

You do not need to wait until you menstruate or ovulate or your cycles return to their pre-Pill length. Furthermore, irregularity of cycles before you commenced taking the Pill is not a problem since you learn to assess your fertility day by day.

Charting

You will need to keep a daily record of any discharge for two to four weeks while avoiding intercourse and all genital contact. This will ensure that your mucus pattern is not obscured by seminal fluid or vaginal secretions associated with intercourse. A month is sufficient to obtain the necessary information to apply the method whether your fertility has returned or not, or whether you have a period or not.

It will become apparent from your pattern whether you are fertile or infertile. (See p. 41, where the charting is described.) A chart of a woman who stopped taking the Pill is illustrated in Figure 9, p. 132.

What to expect after stopping the Pill

Within a few days of discontinuing the Pill, you will bleed as you normally do after each cycle of the Pill (withdrawal bleed). This is due to the sudden removal of the Pill's synthetic hormones. The lining of the uterus grows in response to the synthetic hormones and is usually shed when these are discontinued.

The next time you bleed may be about one month later. However, not all women menstruate so soon. There is no way of predicting how long it will take *your* body to return to normal and your natural ovulatory cycles to resume. For most women ovulation usually returns after a few cycles. Some may ovulate the first cycle after stopping the Pill: so it is necessary to be watchful for signs of fertility this first month.

Prolonged delays in ovulating occur most commonly among young women using the Pill, and those prone to irregular periods before starting to take the Pill. Although this anovulatory situation is not a threat to health, it makes conception impossible, and suggests a significant metabolic disturbance. Treatment with fertility drugs is often successful in re-starting ovulation and menstruation, and about 50 per cent of women conceive after treatment.[1] As indicated in chapter 12, it is wise to allow at least two years for the natural cycles to resume before contemplating fertility drugs. 'Treating' irregularity by prescribing the Pill is bad medicine and may cause more of the same problems.

The mucus after coming off the Pill

The type of Pill you have been using will affect the mucus pattern that you now see. It is most likely that during the first month of charting you will recognise a discharge that indicates infertility.[2]

This infertile pattern will be one of two types. Either you will see no mucus, and experience dryness, or you will have an unchanging discharge that is sticky and scant, or continuous and wet and that looks milky or watery. Different women have their own ways of describing this discharge; however a characteristic they always notice is its unchanging nature.

Both these situations are described as a Basic Infertile Pattern. The first is a Basic Infertile Pattern of dryness, the second, a Basic Infertile Pattern of discharge. This discharge that signals *infertility* remains the same day after day, without change.

Some women experience a wet discharge that varies significantly from day to day. In such circumstances it is advisable to have a medical examination as this type of mucus may be caused by a damaged cervix, requiring treatment. Guidance by a teacher is helpful.

The first ovulation after coming off the Pill

Initially, the body may make several attempts to ovulate, and these are recognisable by a change from the Basic Infertile Pattern. The hormone levels may rise and fall again without reaching the level necessary for ovulation. Each rise is associated with a mucus change.

The change may take the form of an altered sensation at the vulva or the appearance of discharge, or the occurrence of bleeding. You will know you have not ovulated because of the failure to menstruate within eleven to sixteen days of such changes.

Because any of these changes could lead to ovulation, it is important to observe the guidelines described in the following pages. Often the first ovulation after coming off the Pill is accompanied by abdominal pain, severe in some women. However, pain is an unreliable indicator of ovulation, and should not be allowed to contradict your mucus signals.

As you become more aware of your individual mucus pattern, the BIP discharge—whether flaky, sticky, cloudy, or wet, and the same day after day—can be distinguished from any mucus that is different. Recognition of the initial infertile pattern, and avoidance of intercourse during—and for three days after—a change in the pattern, will enable you to see your fertility return without conceiving. Bleeding indicates a change, so follow the same rules—wait while it is present and for three days after. Most women using the Billings Method for the first time after taking the Pill will need a few normal cycles to be able to recognise confidently the Peak of fertility. The interval between ovulation and menstruation is often short for a few cycles, indicating inadequate ovulation and infertility.

Applying the method

After the initial two to four weeks' charting and, if possible, with the guidance of an experienced teacher to help you interpret your pattern, you will be in a position to apply the method. The guidelines for avoiding a pregnancy are:

MENSTRUATION   Avoid intercourse and all genital contact on days of heavy bleeding. (The bleeding may obscure fertile mucus with fertile characteristics, which may occur during menstruation in short cycles.) If you do not recognise mucus with fertile characteristics and a Peak prior to bleeding, avoid intercourse for three days following bleeding, and continue the Early Day Rules.

THE BASIC INFERTILE PATTERN (BIP)   During dry days or days of your characteristic BIP discharge, alternate evenings are available for intercourse. If ovulation is delayed, you will experience a lengthy time during which these Early Day Rules are applied. By leaving a gap of a day after intercourse you ensure that your mucus pattern is not obscured by seminal fluid or vaginal secretions associated with intercourse. Use of the night for intercourse, rather than the early morning or day, enables you to form an accurate assessment of your fertility through mucus observations during the day.

THE CHANGE   On any day of mucus that differs from your characteristic infertile pattern, or when bleeding occurs, avoid intercourse then, and for three days afterwards. If no Peak has been identified, continue confining intercourse to alternate evenings.

THE PEAK   The Peak of fertility is the last day of slipperiness at the vulva, whether the mucus can be seen or not. The greatest quantity of mucus with strings or loops appears one or two days before the Peak. On the day after the Peak, stickiness or dryness will be observed and the vulval swelling will quickly diminish.

After you recognise both the mucus with fertile characteristics and the Peak, allow a gap of three days. Thereafter, until your next menstrual period, intercourse day or night as desired will carry no risk of a pregnancy.

IF YOU ARE USING THE METHOD TO HAVE A CHILD   It is advisable to avoid conception for three or four months after coming off the Pill.[3]

This is because there is a tendency to miscarry for several months after using contraceptive hormones. However, those pregnancies that do not miscarry usually proceed normally.

Your chances of achieving a pregnancy are maximised by timing intercourse to coincide with the fertile mucus Peak. (See chapter 12.)

'I stopped taking the Pill because my husband and I wanted to start a family.

We were warned not to attempt to conceive for some months to avoid the possibility of a miscarriage. During this time we learned and practised the Billings Method.

I didn't see any fertile mucus until two months after coming off the Pill; but when it came I had no trouble picking it. Just like clockwork, I had my first menstrual period thirteen days later.

My fertility was back and I felt like cheering. Not only could

I have a child, but I felt excited about my new knowledge of how my body worked.'

Post-Pill infertility

The first pills contained a high dose of oestrogens that very effectively abolished ovulation. Modern pills have a lower dose of oestrogen and progestogen, or solely progestogen. They block ovulation only in some cycles. The efficiency of these pills depends, rather, on the contraceptive effect of the cervix producing a mucus impenetrable to sperm and causing a disuse shrinkage of the upper part of the cervix that normally produces mucus favourable to sperm. This effect often lasts for a long time after the Pill is stopped, and accounts for much of the post-Pill infertility *even after the woman returns to ovulating normally.* If pregnancy is desired, patience is sometimes required for two to three years while nature restores the cervix to normal.

The disruption of endometrial function caused by the Pill results in the failure of implantation of the embryo if conception has not been prevented. This explains some miscarriages that occur in the first few months after stopping the Pill. Chromosomal abnormalities have explained other miscarriages following the Pill.

Those women wishing to use the Billings Method after discontinuing Depo Provera (p. 189) or Norplant (p. 192) are recommended to contact an accredited teacher and learn to chart. A Basic Infertile Pattern will usually be recognised quickly and the Early Day Rules can be applied if the concern is to avoid pregnancy. The return of fertility is usually greatly delayed.

The method in the balance

Many women who give up the Pill do so after the age of thirty-five when the risk of side-effects increases. These potential risks to health include thrombosis, heart attacks, and high blood pressure. The most recent studies point to cancer of ovary, breast and cervix in women of all ages.

Couples may then feel themselves plunged into a dilemma about fertility control. Should they change to another artificial method of contraception which may disrupt the body's rhythms; or can a natural method provide the solution?

The prospect of some days of abstinence may require some readjustment for a couple used to the Pill. Times of abstinence necessary to avoid pregnancy are, however, compensated for by days of complete sexual freedom.

The temptation to increase the opportunities for intercourse by using barrier contraceptive methods during the fertile phase instead of making full use of infertile days should be resisted, particularly if there is an important reason to avoid pregnancy. Any genital contact, whether barriers are used or not, will confuse the mucus pattern, and increase the possibility of a pregnancy at the fertile time.

Switching to the Billings Method brings with it many benefits to health. During the initial month of charting and in the following months, you will probably notice that any vaginal infections clear up. These are commonly associated with Pill use.

Many women experience a psychological lift and an immediate improvement in their moods, for the Pill may contribute to irritability, depression, headaches, and loss of libido.

It is not uncommon to hear women who have changed to the Billings Method after being on the Pill talk of a deep satisfaction at tuning into the rhythm of their cycles for the first time. By understanding your fertility, you build up a store of valuable knowledge of your body that will be of benefit for the whole of your fertile life.

'After six years on the Pill, and having developed blood clots in my legs, I was strongly advised by my doctor to come off the Pill. This left us in a difficult situation. My husband and I long ago had decided that our family of three was as many as we could cope with. The prospect of an unreliable method of contraception was extremely upsetting and stressful for us both. Then we heard about the Billings Method. Until I became confident about recognising my mucus signals, it was difficult and unsettling. But after a few months when my cycles were back to normal and I was confident in my ability to interpret my mucus, I was far happier and more relaxed than I had been for years.'

A remarkable increase in knowledge and concern is noted in husbands and partners who gladly accept their part and co-operate with their wives.

CHAPTER **10**

Breastfeeding and the Billings Method

Breastfeeding and the Billings Method complement each other. Mother, father and baby all benefit.

After birth, most women experience a period of natural infertility, prolonged for months or even years if a mother breastfeeds her baby. Nature's plan seems to enable you to care for your baby without the demands of another pregnancy too soon. But once the need for your milk diminishes, your body responds by ovulating.

The Billings Method enables you to recognise the months of infertility, so that you can enjoy a sexual relationship free from contraceptive devices or anxiety about the possible effects of the hormones in the Pill on your milk and your baby.

Ovulation is likely to occur before your first menstruation, so it is extremely important to develop as early as possible an awareness of the mucus that signals ovulation.

In the same way, women who are not breastfeeding following a birth, or who have suffered a miscarriage, can use their mucus signals to recognise the shift from infertility to fertility. Fertility usually returns within six weeks of the birth if the baby is not breastfed.

'I found it a great relief to be free from worry about condoms, diaphragms, IUDs, or the Pill, while my baby and I were getting to know each other, and the family was making the inevitable adjustments following a birth.'

'Looking back on all those months, I wish I had known about the Billings Method. We used everything and I was infertile all the time.'

Breastfeeding and the Pill

For many years the Pill in various forms, and contraceptive injections, have been given to large numbers of breastfeeding mothers. Small amounts of the hormones have been identified in the baby's blood during breastfeeding when the mother is taking contraceptive medication in various forms. Harmful effects on the development of the child have been feared. The end of the rapid brain growth does not occur until six to nine months after birth.[1] Breast milk of poor quality and quantity has been reported with the use of synthetic hormones taken by mouth, injection or implants.[2]

Other drugs may also impair the quality of breast milk. The avoidance of all drugs, if possible, during breastfeeding is a healthy practice.

How long are you likely to be infertile while breastfeeding?

The number of months you will be infertile will depend on several factors, including the extent to which your baby demands your breast milk, and on your physical and psychological make-up.

A study of eighty breastfeeding mothers has shown that those who allow the baby to depend on breast milk entirely for nutrition for six months and partially breastfeed thereafter, and who also use the breast as a pacifier, are not likely to ovulate for twelve months after birth.[3]

In Africa, the continuation of breastfeeding of children up to about the age of five in short bursts during the day and at night, enables births to be spaced naturally at intervals of about four years.[4]

Another study of returning fertility after childbirth and during lactation involved fifty-five women. It was carried out by measurement of urinary oestrogen, pregnanediol excretion and cervical mucus production, and showed that none bled before fifteen weeks and one-third did so before six months. When the first bleed occurred, within six weeks of delivery, 50 per cent were anovulatory, 30 per cent had short or deficient luteal phases, and 17 per cent were normal ovulatory cycles.[5]

In this study the mothers did not adhere to the strict breastfeeding regime. This is a realistic experience. Every mother and every baby–mother relationship is individual. The phenomenon of short luteal phases after giving birth was first reported by Brown in 1956.[6] This was later shown, by Gross and Eastman,[7] to be linked with elevated prolactin levels.

If solids are introduced within the first few months of life, or if mothers are particularly anxious about their breast milk supply, or if the supply of breast milk diminishes for any reason, ovulation is likely to occur sooner.

The key to successful fertility control is to make no assumptions, leave nothing to chance. Watch your mucus carefully, and observe the Billings Method guidelines.

LAM (Lactational Amenorrhoea Method)

The value of breastfeeding for the baby's wellbeing as well as its benefits to the mother in assisting the uterus to return to normal and helping to protect her from breast cancer in the future is now well recognised. More and more clearly it has been realised, too, that breastfeeding can provide natural child-spacing, and it is therefore being increasingly urged. This is good news for public health.

A WHO study on breastfeeding assessed its effect on fertility control. Reports have shown that a LAM regime—full breastfeeding for six months, during which time there is no bleeding—has a pregnancy rate of 2 per cent. Some claim a lower rate.

However, the instructions to ignore mucus signs in the LAM studies meant foregoing the advantages of the Billings Method. If women learnt the patterns of infertility in the early weeks of breastfeeding, the pregnancy rate noted by the LAM studies could have been avoided. Not all women meet the criteria of total breastfeeding, as has been shown, and will at any time exhibit evidence of returning fertility by either mucus or bleeding, which are readily recognised and dealt with through application of the Billings Method guidelines.

The Ovarian Meter (see p. 215) will likewise demonstrate infertility by low oestrogens in the early weeks of breastfeeding, and by a rise in oestrogens will forecast impending fertility, thereby providing a perfect correlation with Billings Method observations and guidelines.

The early training in making observations and recognising the signs of returning fertility after the unchanging pattern of the Basic Infertile Pattern provides excellent experience for continuing natural fertility regulation when cycles return; it is also invaluable in later years when infertility becomes increasingly obvious at the approach to the menopause. No one with a breastfeeding experience of fertility regulation need fear the menopause.

After six months, or if there is any bleeding, or if other

food or fluids are introduced to the baby, the Lactation Amenorrhoea Method is no longer applicable. The experienced user of the Billings Method will be able to recognise continuing infertility if this is the case, and can continue to breastfeed confidently while applying the guidelines.[8]

What causes this infertility during the breastfeeding period?

Oestrogens are at a low level while you are breastfeeding. This is due to the effect of the hormone prolactin, which controls breast milk production.

Over time, the pituitary gland at the base of the brain starts to switch off prolactin production. Gradually the hormone cycle leading to ovulation takes over. This may occur in a series of stop/start events, as if the body is trying to ovulate. These hormone fluctuations will be reflected in changes in your mucus. Do not presume the first bleeding you see is menstruation. Light bleeding or spotting may be due to a rise in oestrogen coinciding with ovulation and a return of fertility, or it may be a withdrawal bleed caused by a fall in oestrogen.

Breast milk production

Sucking sets in motion a reflex chain of events along nerve pathways involving the brain, the pituitary gland and the breasts. The hormone oxytocin is released from the pituitary and causes the 'let-down' reflex. This involves a flow of milk from the nipple as special cells around the milk ducts contract. The sight, smell or thought of the baby can initiate this very sensitive reflex.

Prolactin, which is responsible for the continuing production of milk, has already been at work, in conjunction with oestrogen and progesterone, causing growth of glandular breast tissue in preparation for feeding. This hormone continues to operate in response to the baby's sucking.

The sucking skill of the baby develops at the same time as breast growth during pregnancy. Pictures of a fourteen-week-old foetus often show the thumb being sucked. In this way tiny cheek and mouth muscles are exercised, and the complicated sucking mechanism practised.

Instant and vigorous sucking by the baby when put to the breast after birth often leads to parents to exclaim that their child 'knows what to do'. In fact, the baby has been practising for months. Mothers feeling they ought to stop thumb-sucking should realise they are dealing with a long-standing habit.

After birth, if mothers wish to breastfeed, it is desirable that they have access to their babies for feeding according to need. The practice of sedating mothers for a prolonged period to ensure sleep, together with injudicious additions of breast-milk substitutes in the hospital nursery, has been the cause of many breastfeeding failures. Breasts engorged with milk after a long sleep cannot be emptied by a baby who is not hungry, and soon an over-abundance of milk is converted to an inadequate supply. The milk supply is further threatened if a mother becomes anxious when she is told she has 'not enough milk' by a nurse who is conducting test feeds. 'Why bother?' a friend or relative may ask. And the baby goes home on the bottle.

Breast milk is tailor-made for the baby's needs. For the first few feeds, a substance called colostrum is produced by the breasts. This prepares the baby's digestive tract for later milk, and supplies important antibodies to protect against infection. Breastfeeding helps protect the baby from developing allergies to foreign proteins in these first few weeks when the digestive tract is vulnerable. Colostrum is also of benefit to the delicate skin of the nipples, and should not be washed away with soap and water.

Patterns of discharge during infertility

By careful observation, you can learn to recognise your Basic Infertile Pattern while you are breastfeeding.

It doesn't matter if you have not used the Billings Method before—you can learn to recognise your infertile pattern by making daily observations.

If you are infertile, your pattern may be:
- Dry all the time—nothing to see
- The same discharge day after day
- Days of unchanging discharge interspersed with dry days. In this case the characteristics of the discharge remain the same. After observing for two weeks it can be seen that every time the discharge appears it is the same kind of discharge. While the discharge may vary from woman to woman, the key to its recognition is its *unchanging pattern.*

Thus a woman may notice a milky, wet discharge every day for months on end. Another woman may record flaky, dry or sticky discharge which becomes very familiar as it is noticed each day. Awareness becomes second nature and changes can be picked up and evaluated in relation to the now familiar Basic Infertile Pattern. This discharge forms in the vagina and is not mucus.

During this prolonged phase of infertility, couples may need new insights about how to achieve satisfying intercourse. One common problem is an excessively dry vagina due to reduced production of mucus by the cervix. This can be overcome by an unhurried and loving preparation for intercourse, which allows the vagina to produce lubricating secretions.

It is valuable to realise that intercourse does not depend solely on a raised level of oestrogen hormone to be

emotionally and physically satisfying; loving consideration between partners is extremely important. Sensitive
nervous reflexes operate which are dependent upon emotional as well as physical stimulation.

Especially loving preparation for intercourse is helpful
during the menopause later in life, when a similar
dryness may occur. It can readily be seen how the successful management of the infertility of breastfeeding can
be a good preparation for menopause when oestrogens
are also low.

Charting

You should begin to keep a record of your discharge from
three weeks after the birth when blood loss (lochia) tends
to stop. (See p. 41, where the method of charting is
explained.) Even though infertility may continue for a
considerable time, charting is recommended because it
increases your awareness of the mucus signals so that any
change is readily noticed. You become familiar with a
pattern that indicates infertility.

While charting, it is helpful to describe your mucus
observations and sensations in your own words. Also
record the number of feeds each day, the longest interval
between feeds, any alteration in the feeding routine or
sickness, teething and irritability of the baby. This will
help you (and a Billings Method teacher, if one is available) to assess accurately the state of your fertility.

Mothers of young babies who are fully breastfed,
thriving and contented and where the breast is used as a
pacifier or comforter, are unlikely to be fertile. If your
baby is dependent entirely on your milk for nutrition, is
sucking frequently, and on demand, you will probably
not ovulate or menstruate for several months.

Under these circumstances you can safely have intercourse according to inclination, apart from the days

excluded by the Early Day Rules (p. 47). These include the day following love-making, when your mucus pattern may be obscured by seminal fluid or vaginal secretions associated with intercourse, as well as any days of bleeding, or days when there is any change in the pattern.

If you are partially breastfeeding, or your baby is three months or older, or your periods have returned, you will need to *defer intercourse for two or three weeks while charting*, in order to gain a clear picture of your discharge pattern, and thus of your state of fertility.

After this, if your pattern indicates that you are still infertile, you can safely have intercourse on alternate nights. It is also advisable to confine intercourse to the evenings so that your assessment of fertility is based on a full day's observations (for the fertile mucus may begin during the early hours of the morning before it is apparent to you).

Some couples attempt to gain more opportunities for intercourse by using a condom or diaphragm without allowing a clear day following intercourse. However intercourse with these devices will result in secretions which may obscure your mucus pattern.

The chart showing the return to fertility of a woman breastfeeding her baby is illustrated on p. 134.

The return of fertility

Any change in your pattern, or any bleeding, may signal a change in your hormone balance and a return of fertility, even if you are fully breastfeeding.

You need to be particularly observant for changes in the pattern when:
• Night feeds are discontinued
• Complementary feeds with infant milk formulas are introduced
• Solids are included in your baby's diet

- Your baby's feeding pattern is altered due to sickness or irritability, such as during teething
- Weaning is taking place, and afterwards.

All these events may trigger hormonal changes which set in train the process of ovulation, mucus from the cervix and thus the return of fertility.

Bleeding will signify the rise and fall of oestrogens even before ovulation. Oestrogen stimulates the growth of the endometrium, which will be shed when the oestrogen level falls again. Sometimes high oestrogen will trigger ovulation and be closely preceded by some bleeding. Sometimes there will be repeated bleeds before ovulation occurs ('anovulatory cycles'). This tends to be the case if bleeding occurs within the first nine months after birth.[9] The first bleed you experience may be quite heavy.

You may experience cycles with a post-ovulatory phase of less than eleven days. These cycles are infertile. The reason for this shortened interval between the mucus Peak and the next menstrual period may be a raised level of the hormone prolactin, which stimulates milk production, preventing a full development of ovulation. Soon after ovulation resumes, your cycles will usually return to a familiar length.

The first sign of any change in your state of fertility may be intermittent days of mucus interrupting a Basic Infertile Pattern of dryness. You may not ovulate, for your body may be 'practising' for the full return of fertility.

If you are watching your mucus, you will usually be warned of the return of fertility well in advance. A study of forty-two breastfeeding mothers showed that thirty-eight had six or more days of fertile-type mucus (i.e. the slippery sensation without visible mucus) before ovulation, which was confirmed by hormone measurements.[10]

If the mucus changes, the safest approach is to avoid intercourse on these days of changed mucus and for three days afterwards. This is also the best policy for any day of spotting or bleeding which will tinge the mucus with blood, giving it a pink or brown appearance.

Some women begin regular menstruation early (within the first six weeks) even while breastfeeding totally. Recognition of the mucus pattern and application of the guidelines will enable you to control your fertility in this situation.

If in doubt about possible fertility, it is wise to wait and watch for a few weeks. This period of abstinence presents little problem if couples are prepared for it, and it is usually readily accepted because of the freedom and security made possible by the Billings Method in the preceding months.

When ovulation finally occurs it will be associated with the slippery mucus. If the cycle is fertile, menstruation will occur eleven to sixteen days after ovulation. By carefully observing your mucus signals, this first menstruation after birth can be predicted accurately; an encouraging sign that you are mastering the method.

Maintaining your milk supply

Sometimes babies themselves seem to be aware of the body's attempts to ovulate. They may become irritable and show less inclination for breast milk close to ovulation, when the taste and smell of the milk alter. Menstruation also seems to be associated with some protest by the baby.

Many mothers notice that they are producing less breast milk than usual when their babies are about three months old. The baby's weight gain is suspended, and signs of returning fertility—such as intermittent days of lubricative mucus—may become evident.

Introducing solids or canned baby foods or extra milk at this stage may prematurely halt your milk production. This is the time for some mothering of mother. It is often very helpful if those who are close to you can enable you to devote all your time and attention to your baby. Twenty-four hours in bed, with frequent breastfeeds, is invaluable if you are to maintain your milk supply.

With frequent breastfeeds, extra fluids, nourishing food and rest, the flow of breast milk improves and again becomes adequate. This postpones the onset of fertility and the infertile pattern returns. Once past this three-month hurdle, breastfeeding usually returns to normal, and infertility is prolonged.

Another episode like this frequently occurs when babies are about nine months old. If you and your baby wish to continue breastfeeding at this stage, increased opportunities for sucking and a few days rest usually provide the key.

It is now generally accepted that the introduction of solids should be delayed until four to six months. As long as you are well nourished and your baby is gaining weight, happy and contented, there is no need to introduce solids until the baby is six months old, an age that usually coincides with the baby's first teeth.

The 'educational diet'

The need for an 'educational diet' is often made obvious by babies themselves.

At about five months of age, they often show interest in the various tastes and textures of foods that others are eating. Small amounts of solids introduced into your baby's diet will not greatly alter your mucus pattern, as long as the baby's fluid and main caloric requirements are met by breast milk. These eating experiences, which are social as well as educational, are preparing babies to accept adult food with pleasure later on.

Nutritionally speaking, milk should remain the most important component of a baby's diet for nine months to a year. Some babies resist the introduction of other food and prefer to go on sucking. Babies display individual behaviour, and some seem to require substantial amounts of solid food for months before others.

Weaning

The return of fertility may be prompted by a reduced number of feeds, as the baby is given or demands additional food and other fluids. It may also closely follow any ill health you or your child experience when either insufficient breast milk, or inadequate demand, leads to a reduction of breast milk production.

The effect of weaning on the mucus pattern differs from woman to woman. If weaning is gradual, or the baby is encouraged to wean himself or herself, there may be several patches of mucus with fertile characteristics before ovulation occurs. For a short time the pattern may be confusing. The sensible solution is to postpone intercourse temporarily until the pattern is clear.

Once weaning is completed ovulation usually follows quickly; this is recognisable by the presence of the fertile mucus and the Peak. Note particularly the change in sensation. Not every woman will *see* abundant mucus.

'I fed my baby for three months. Then he became very cross and cried a lot. I was using the Billings Method and after a few weeks I suddenly had a period. That was the beginning of the end. The baby refused my milk and I put him on some bottle feeds. He seemed so hungry. I then noticed a lot of mucus. The baby kept refusing the breast. The mucus stopped. I knew I was going to have a period—which I did. By this time there was very little breast milk left, so I finished feeding. My cycles then returned to normal. I was told I could have persevered with more frequent feeds, as babies sometimes act in this way at about three months especially when

mucus, or bleeding, returns. Next time I will try to encourage more sucking. I am sorry that I had to stop so soon. It wasn't hard to pick my Peak and to understand what was happening with my fertility even though it was the first time I had really noticed mucus.'

Applying the mucus guidelines

Until now, you will have been using guidelines that apply to an infertile pattern. With the return of ovulation and menstruation it is necessary to learn to recognise the Peak of fertility and to apply the Peak rule.

Charting for a month without intercourse will enable you to interpret your pattern accurately, and will provide information about your fertility which will be of benefit for the rest of your fertile life.

Sometimes when cycles begin, a pattern of discharge which indicated infertility while you were breastfeeding will now be replaced by something quite different. For example, a Basic Infertile Pattern of continuous discharge may now be replaced by a Basic Infertile Pattern of dry days. The important point here is that a type of discharge that indicated infertility while you were breastfeeding does not necessarily indicate the same thing once normal cycles have returned.

This is a new set of circumstances, which is why a month of charting without intercourse is necessary.

After the initial month of charting your mucus pattern, continue daily observations and apply the guidelines:

- Avoid intercourse on days of bleeding.
- Use alternate nights for intercourse during the BIP.
- Avoid intercourse as soon as mucus becomes apparent, and for three days following the return of the BIP. This three-day margin allows the pattern to become either obviously fertile, or to indicate infertility.
- When the Peak symptom is recognised, postpone

intercourse for three more days. After this the rest of the cycle is available day or night.

'My first period arrived when my first child—Mary—was sixteen weeks old. By the time she was weaned at nine months, I'd had four cycles; the first lasting forty-three days, then thirty-nine days, thirty-eight days, and thirty-six days. As soon as the weaning was complete, I reverted to my usual cycle of twenty-eight days. Mary had slept through the night from ten weeks, and had started an educational diet at three-and-a-half months.

Having successfully fed Mary, I didn't doubt my ability to do the same with Lucy. However, I underestimated the demands of a two-year-old when trying to breastfeed a new baby.

Lucy had nothing but breast milk until she was six months old. I started weaning her at eight months, and it was then that I got my first period. Forty-three days later I had my second period. From then on my cycles returned to the usual length.

When Lucy was three, Loretta arrived on the scene. I learned the Billings Method while breastfeeding her. She turned out to be a child that scarcely ever slept. Her consistent pattern was little feeds often. She reminded me of Pavlov's dogs—every time the telephone rang she regarded it as feed time.

This frequent sucking had the effect of keeping me infertile for seventeen-and-a-half months. I didn't introduce her to solids until she was six months old, and until that time I didn't note any mucus symptoms at all; from then on I occasionally had patches.

It was interesting to note that when Loretta was twelve months old we had a caravan holiday for two weeks. Because she was fidgety in the car whilst travelling, I fed her much more frequently throughout that two weeks and, as a result, I had a fortnight entirely free of mucus.

However, when the holiday was over and we settled back to normal, I started to get patches of mucus from time to time. I was able to predict my first period by recognising the Peak *symptom after two years without menstruating, including the time of my pregnancy.*

Around the time my periods returned, Loretta gave up nursing in the day time, but continued to nurse at bedtime for another twelve months or so. Eventually at two-and-a-half years, she and I had a long talk and finally she agreed to wean.'

CHAPTER 11

Approaching the menopause

Woman is rare among creatures in that she outlives her reproductive capacity.

From the age of about fifty, most women are infertile, with thirty or so years of life remaining. The change from fertility to infertility is usually gradual, occurring over a number of years. This period of change, the 'climacteric', is commonly marked by menstrual cycles that are extremely variable in length, and by mucus episodes that are increasingly less frequent.

The climacteric often presents problems for a woman and her husband. Irregularity of cycles as the menopause approaches has caused some couples to abstain from intercourse for months or even years. This creates severe stress on relationships, resulting in feelings of rejection and confusion for both.

Sometimes contraceptive medication is used for the first time. Or sterilisation is undertaken, or a hysterectomy accepted on the most slender of gynaecological indications . . . *all at a time when a woman is infertile most of the time and soon to be totally infertile.*

At the menopause, a woman can be overwhelmed by feelings of worthlessness, and she may view the future without enthusiasm. She may become withdrawn and introspective, feeling that nobody cares much about her. A partner may find it simpler to go his own way, not realising that her outbursts are a cry for help, and that a gift or extra attention would be appreciated greatly—especially if he could also encourage her to discuss her problems and anxieties in an atmosphere of loving understanding.

At such a time a woman may see the need to adjust her role, both in society and the family. She may not feel very interesting, because people seem less interested in her. She may put on weight and feel lethargic and unattractive. Sexual inclination may decline due to physical causes. Heavy periods may result in anaemia, fatigue and depression. Falling oestrogens may have caused dryness of the vagina tending to make intercourse painful, and some women experience hot flushes and associated sleep difficulties. It is not uncommon now for sexual problems which have been suppressed during the active, reproductive years to come to the surface, the scales having been tipped by these unpleasant physical experiences. There may be feelings of inadequacy with an overlay of guilt. Very often the lines of communication have come adrift and some of the problems are purely imaginary. It may be that her partner is more demanding for intercourse because he feels that he is losing his youth, or because she is refusing him and therefore seems to be unloving. This paradoxical situation of poor satisfaction followed by increased sexual demands results in misunderstanding on both sides.

On the other hand there may be increased sexual inclination on the woman's part, and the couple must adjust to this.

Loving communication between partners can overcome many difficulties. Other positive steps to overcome problems of the menopause are discussed later in this chapter. Of course, in many instances couples adjust happily to the new situation.

It is impossible and misleading to generalise. For while

the menopausal years may bring some problems, many women find opportunities for a creative and fulfilling lifestyle with major family responsibilities over, worries about an unexpected pregnancy eliminated, and with more time to follow their own interests.

The Billings Method in the pre-menopause

The Billings Method of fertility control can provide security during this time of changing fertility.

If a woman has not used the Billings Method before, this need not prove an obstacle.

It is not necessary to predict the end of fertility: the key to successful fertility regulation at this stage is *positive recognition of the infertility* which will eventually become absolute.

A woman can recognise whether she is fertile or infertile from her cervical mucus. If any difficulties arise, a skilled teacher of the method, or another woman who has successfully used the method, will be able to help her through this time of irregularity.

'At forty-five, with my cycles becoming increasingly long and irregular, my life seemed to be turning into a monstrous game of roulette. Would a chance pregnancy result from an occasional act of love-making? I wondered anxiously.

My doctor cheerfully told me that I couldn't conceive even if I tried. But when I consulted another doctor he advised the Pill.

When I heard about the Billings Method I did not think I could use it because of the lack of any apparent mucus pattern. I could recall mucus resembling raw egg-white occurring perhaps two years ago, but certainly not in recent times.

By keeping a careful record for the next four weeks and by being alert to my mucus subsequently, I knew that I was infertile. This knowledge has given me a new peace of mind and release from unnecessary abstinence.'

Events leading to the menopause

The decline of fertility usually occurs gradually as the functions of the ovaries and cervix change. Most available eggs have matured and left the ovary and although the lining of the uterus may continue to build up and break away and bleeding may continue for months or years due to fluctuating hormone levels, ovulation is occurring less and less frequently.

Statistically, once you reach middle age you are in an age group of low fertility. For example, according to a 1996 World Health Organisation report, up to ten in every 100 women aged forty to forty-four who are not using any method of family planning may become pregnant. For similar but slightly older women, the chances of pregnancy are less, with two or three in every 100 women not using family planning becoming pregnant when aged from forty-five to forty-nine years of age.[1] As women turn fifty and over, pregnancy rates fall progressively to zero.

Typical patterns of changing fertility

The physiological patterns of the pre-menopause vary from woman to woman. However some experiences are common. These include the following:
• Menstrual periods may stop without warning and not begin again. The menopause is the name given to the end of the menstrual periods.
• Cycles may become extremely irregular and vary in length from as short as seventeen days to six months or more; and the amount of menstrual bleeding may likewise vary considerably.

- Ovulation may occur infrequently, although bleeding episodes may continue. Do not rely on bleeding as a guide to your fertility. 'Periods' may continue for months or years beyond your ability to conceive.
- Production of mucus with fertile characteristics by the cervix may stop, even though you may still be ovulating and menstruating. The absence of this mucus means that you are infertile since it is essential if the sperm cells are to retain their fertilising capacity and reach the egg.
- The nutritive lining of the uterus—the endometrium—may be shed within eleven days of the Peak. This premature breakdown of the endometrium—resulting in an infertile cycle—is due to a fall in hormones produced by the corpus luteum (p. 26). An imperfect ovulation is the probable explanation.

Variations between women

The length of the menopause and the severity of associated conditions vary considerably between women. It may extend over months or years, during which fertility may seem to disappear, only to return again months later.

It is impossible to predict when your fertility will finally end, although your pattern may be similar to that of your mother and sisters. The time of the menopause is not related to when your menstrual periods first began, or to the number of children you have.

Assessing your state of fertility

A full medical history will indicate your state of fertility. Factors to be taken into account include:
- Age. If you are forty-five or older you are statistically much less likely to become pregnant.
- Number of children and miscarriages. This is some indication of overall fertility.

- Age of youngest child. This indicates when you were last proven to be fertile. But it does not necessarily tell you anything about subsequent fertility.
- Previous fertility control methods used. Women who have used the Pill and IUD tend to become infertile earlier.
- Recent lengths of menstrual cycles, compared with those you experienced five or ten years ago.
- Approximate date of the onset of irregularity of the cycles.
- Changes in menstrual bleeding, such as reduced or prolonged blood loss, or the presence of blood clots associated with heavy bleeding. Excessive bleeding may cause anaemia and consequent fatigue. Painful periods may have once been the rule. Now many or all are painless.
- Bleeding between periods. This is more common in long pre-menopausal cycles. It sometimes coincides with ovulation, and may be an unfamiliar experience.
- Changes in breast pain or tenderness. Breast tenderness may become very severe, disturbing sleep and lasting for two or three weeks in any particular cycle; or if previously you have been accustomed to a feeling of soreness, fullness and lumpiness in the breasts for a few days before menstruation, this may no longer occur. The disappearance of this breast tension can often be related to a decline in the production of mucus with fertile characteristics.
- A temperature record may indicate, by absence of a rise, that ovulation is not occurring in certain cycles.
- Hot flushes. These are brief events, during which a feeling of heat suddenly rises up the body to the head, producing redness of the neck and face and generalised perspiration, which quickly subside. The flushes may occur as many as thirty times a day, and then disappear for several weeks. Or they may not occur at all. They

may happen during the day or night, in severe cases causing drenching perspiration and disturbed sleep. Although they are associated with low levels of oestrogen (the oestrogen level rises at ovulation) and therefore indicate a day of infertility, they are not a reliable guide to the end of fertility.

- Changes in other familiar signs of ovulation such as the feeling of fullness around the vulva at the time of ovulation, or abdominal pain associated with ovulation, may disappear. This suggests that ovulation is not occurring.
- Recent weight gain. This is commonly associated with declining fertility; but it may be exaggerated by emotional factors such as depression and lethargy, leading to over-eating.
- Changes in the physical characteristics of the cervical mucus. An infertile mucus pattern or dry days increasingly replaces the mucus with fertile characteristics. Women who know the Billings Method say 'The Peak is not as clear as it was'. This is to be expected and is not a reason to look for a back-up method of contraception. It is now that you learn to recognise your *infertility*.

The discharge during the menopause

You may experience dry days for weeks or months, or scanty amounts of dense discharge which does not change. Typically, the pre-menopausal discharge pattern indicates infertility by *remaining unchanged day after day.*

In some women the discharge is sparse or non-existent, producing a dry sensation. Or it may be crumbly, cloudy, yellow, flaky, clotty, craggy, or even watery and continuous, without ever developing the lubricative qualities of cervical mucus. Every woman experiences an individual pattern of infertility which she can learn to recognise.

It is common for dry days to increase in number, and for whole cycles or months to pass during which no mucus is seen or felt. Any return of possible fertility will be mirrored by your mucus. If you are fertile, the fertile characteristics of the mucus will be evident by the sensation it produces and your observations of it.

Learning to recognise infertility—keeping a record of discharges

The first step is to keep a daily record of your mucus pattern for about a month, avoiding intercourse and genital contact during this time. This ensures that your mucus pattern is not obscured by seminal fluid or vaginal secretions associated with intercourse.

It is not necessary to wait for menstruation before beginning your chart. You may never have another period.

A chart of a woman approaching the menopause is illustrated on p. 135. Don't be disturbed if a mucus pattern typical of a fertile cycle is not apparent. Your pattern is more likely to indicate infertility. Don't wait for the Peak symptom. There may never be one. Simply record your sensations and what you see in your own words; a Billings Method teacher will help you interpret the pattern if need be.

If you are infertile, you will soon learn to recognise your own characteristic infertile pattern; and if you are fertile you will learn to recognise your Peak of fertility (p. 48). Be alert for any *change* in your mucus, which will signal the possibility of fertility.

A month after beginning your chart you will be able to apply the Billings Method guidelines whether or not you have menstruated, and whether you are fertile or infertile.

Some couples who marry late in their reproductive lives may wish to have a family. As a woman's fertility declines steeply after forty, she will need to observe her pattern very carefully in order to make use of her most fertile days, thereby maximising her chances of conceiving.

Guidelines for avoiding a pregnancy

These cover all cycle variations of the pre-menopausal period, and are the same guidelines that apply to other phases of your reproductive life. (For a more complete explanation of the guidelines, see p. 47.)

MENSTRUATION   During menstruation, avoid intercourse and all genital contact on days of heavy bleeding (in case the menstrual blood obscures the mucus which may occur early in very short cycles). If you do not recognise a Peak prior to bleeding, avoid intercourse during, and for three days following, the bleed.

THE BASIC INFERTILE PATTERN   During dry days or days of your characteristic unchanging discharge, use alternate nights for intercourse.

THE CHANGE   On all days of spotty bleeding or mucus that differs from your characteristic infertile pattern avoid intercourse then, and for three days afterwards.

FERTILE MUCUS AND THE PEAK   After you recognise both mucus with fertile characteristics and the Peak, allow a gap of three days after the Peak before resuming intercourse. The combined fertility of you and your partner is then zero, and intercourse day or night until your next menstruation, carries no possibility of a pregnancy.

As time goes by the Peak becomes indefinite because of the increasing failure of the cervix to respond to raised oestrogens. When this happens the Early Day Rules should be applied continuously, that is, intercourse on alternate evenings during the Basic Infertile Pattern. When the pattern changes, that is, when any mucus, spotting or bleeding develops, wait until the change is over and the BIP has been re-established for an extra three days. The simple rule is 'wait and see, 1, 2, 3.'

It is of great importance when making observations to

pay particular attention to the sensations at the vulva, especially as the quantity of mucus usually diminishes considerably. Eventually all mucus and bleeding will cease. It is natural for the oestrogens to rise sometimes very high and fall again successively over several months while the final adjustments are made that result in infertility. When the oestrogens are high the cervix may no longer respond to produce mucus, but the endometrium will respond and bleed both when the level of oestrogens is high and also when it falls again. This irregular bleeding tells the woman that her oestrogens are fluctuating. The fact that hot flushes come for several weeks, vanish for some weeks only to return again, also indicates that the level of the oestrogens is fluctuating. This hormonal adjustment is a normal event and should be allowed to proceed without interference.

Other fertility control methods during the menopause

THE PILL   The longer you use the Pill, the more likely are side-effects (see p. 172). It is apparent that Pill problems still remain in spite of attempts to rectify their shortcomings. Thus the health of women approaching the menopause, like the health of younger women, may be endangered by contraceptive hormones.

The signs of declining fertility will be easily recognised by observing the mucus patterns. However, these signs will not be apparent if you use the Pill because the Pill obscures the normal mucus pattern. Many women put their health at risk for years when, unknown to them, their fertility is over.

THE INTRA-UTERINE DEVICE   The IUD has progressively lost favour with the medical profession because of the serious complications resulting in pelvic inflammatory disease, septic abortions and ectopic pregnancies. These problems have resulted in expensive litigation in many countries with the removal of most of the devices from the market.

STERILISATION, TUBAL LIGATION AND HYSTERECTOMY   The serious side-effects of these procedures when used to control fertility can be easily avoided by a knowledge of naturally declining fertility. Heavy bleeding sometimes follows tubal ligation and it can only be remedied by hysterectomy. Ectopic pregnancies are also a complication of tubal ligation, and it has been reported that the procedure can cause and exacerbate pre-mentrual tension in some women. Hysterectomy should not be undertaken without good reason. Following a hysterectomy, post-operative depression and sexual dysfunction can occur, often involving loss of libido and pain with intercourse, and the fear of loss of femininity.[2]

RHYTHM AND TEMPERATURE METHODS   Both these methods have proved unsatisfactory at the time of menopause.

In a study of ninety-eight pre-menopausal women using the Rhythm Method, seventeen became pregnant at the onset of irregularity.[3] This is because the Rhythm Method depends on cycles being approximately constant in length, or remaining within a range that has been established during nine to twelve months' observation. When cycle durations vary markedly—such as when approaching the menopause—arithmetical calculations of ovulation are bound to fail.

The Temperature Method, which relies on a rise in temperature around the time of ovulation, is also unsatisfactory. This is because ovulation occurs less and less frequently as fertility declines at the menopause. Consequently temperature rises are few and far between and couples may wait needlessly for months or even years for the rise in temperature that signals that ovulation has passed. This is most unsatisfactory for relationships and may engender much unhappiness and confusion.

It is extremely frustrating for couples to realise only in retrospect that a long cycle was infertile—and that they have abstained unnecessarily throughout it. In such a situation they may decide to 'take a chance', with the possibility of an unintended pregnancy. The advantage of the Billings Method in this situation is that it enables positive recognition of infertility, day by day.

Hormone Replacement Therapy (HRT)

The passage of fertility to infertility is a natural event and should not be regarded as an abnormality. There is a physical adjustment during this time when hormone levels fluctuate widely. The pituitary hormone (FSH) rises in an effort to stimulate the ageing ovaries. At times the ovaries produce very large amounts of oestrogen at ovulation, which is becoming less frequent, and also at other times. The uterus responds by bleeding, and while this bleeding persists the woman may consider that she is still fertile even though she may have stopped ovulating some time earlier. The bleeding indicates that she still has relatively high oestrogens.

Expert assessment, common sense and sympathetic management of each individual woman is necessary when hormone therapy is being considered. To give all women hormone replacement therapy routinely is an ill-considered decision. The proportion of women seeking medical help at this time has increased due to public advertising in recent years, which has persuaded many women that they need HRT.

Some of the symptoms of menopause, for example sleep disturbances, irritability, depression, fatigue and painful intercourse will be alleviated easily by simple non-hormonal measures such as rest periods, mild sedatives, and iron treatment for anaemia which may result from heavy bleeding. Recently that useful diagnostic aid,

Professor Brown's Ovarian Meter, by demonstrating the hormonal explanation of unusual bleeding, has spared many women the unnecessary procedures of curettage and hysterectomy.

Hot flushes will come and go as oestrogen levels change from time to time. Therefore, therapy for women who are seriously affected should be intermittent rather than continuous. In the absence of such an approach, many women try HRT. This therapy usually consists of oestrogen combined with regular intervals of progestogen; continuous combined oestrogen and progestogen taken every day; oestrogen alone for women who have had a hysterectomy; or testosterone combined with any of the above. While there is considerable evidence that HRT can relieve hot flushes, there are growing concerns that it may also have serious ill-effects on healthy women, particularly when used for more than several years.[4] The latest advice is that clinicians should stop prescribing combined HRT for long-term use.[5]

HRT will not prevent pregnancy; careful observation and application of the Billings Method guidelines will provide security during a short course of HRT if this is considered necessary.

Alternatives to hormone therapy

It is worth pursuing alternatives to hormone therapy because they do not alter the body's chemistry.

If a woman is happy and content, natural lubrication of the vagina will occur prior to intercourse. Her partner needs to know this and take time in love-making. Then it is unnecessary to use lubricative creams or jellies, or oestrogen creams, all of which disturb the pattern of natural secretions. It is easy to set up a vicious circle: a dry vagina makes intercourse painful; painful intercourse is resisted; and this leads to disharmony and prevents the flow of natural secretions in the vagina.

Sympathetic counselling is often necessary to identify problems that have nothing to do with the menopause but which, by causing anxiety and distress, may worsen menopausal symptoms. Increased efforts to improve communication between partners can help. Husbands benefit greatly from an explanation of the menopause.

Rest each day and attention to general health are important. A woman at this time tends to become much less active. It is most important that regular exercise is taken; healthy muscles help to maintain joints and bones in good condition.

When synthetic oestrogens are taken, the mucus pattern is disturbed (synthetic hormones—by influencing centres in the brain—suppress natural hormones); the cervix produces a discharge which resembles mucus with fertile characteristics and may be blood-stained. Careful observation of isolated days which are all the same and are not slippery, indicating infertility, is necessary.

Symptoms of unusual severity may be alleviated by a natural oestrogen, oestrone sulphate, given in a dose equivalent to a small dose of the more harmful synthetic oestrogens formerly used. A short course only may be necessary. While using this medication, continue to chart and apply the Early Day Rules to the Basic Infertile Pattern.

The use of a progestogen is sometimes helpful in controlling severe bleeding and clotting. This treatment should not be prolonged. The normal physiological development of infertility should be allowed to proceed as naturally as possible.

Progestogen at the menopause

A progestogen (often in the form of the Pill) is sometimes prescribed to pre-menopausal women to make their cycles average-length by prolonging the postovulatory phase (which tends to become shorter as fertility declines). Without good cause, however, this treatment is inadvisable.

The progestogen alters the mucus produced by the cervix, making assessment of fertility very difficult. Through disturbance of the brain-pituitary-ovarian interaction, ovulation is often abolished. Progestogens when used to prolong cycle length can alter the normal development of the endometrium and cause erratic, uncontrollable bleeding. In the unlikely event of implantation occurring, there is a risk of damage to the foetus.

Progestogen may also result in the production of clots that may block vital blood vessels (see p. 173).[6]

The problem of osteoporosis

Reduced bone density, which tends to occur gradually around the menopause, predisposes to fractures with minimal trauma. However, long-term universal use of hormones in treating or attempting to prevent this condition is not recommended.[7]

An assessment of the risk of developing osteoporosis must be made. A family history of fractures and of infrequent irregular menstruation throughout reproductive life is significant. A poor diet, which is high in animal proteins, salt, caffeine and alcohol and low in calcium-rich foods, for example, milk and cheese, may suggest poor bone health. Lack of exercise, low body weight, and heavy cigarette smoking in particular may indicate the development of future bone disorders. Correcting this life-style is advisable, and oestrogen therapy may be considered helpful. It must be borne in mind, however, that sex hormones given to a woman who smokes heavily may be very detrimental to health.

Following the report of the Women's Health Initiative which enrolled more than 160 000 postmenopausal women in the US in clinical trials, the proponents of long-term use of HRT have been forced to re-consider the overblown estimates of its benefits. Hormone therapy is now recommended primarily for short-term use for the relief of menopause-related symptoms such as hot flushes. It is no longer advised for reducing the risk of heart disease or stroke.

Long-term medication with oestrogen alone carries the risk of cancer of the endometrium. As noted earlier, this must be offset by adding a progestogen, which causes a periodic shedding of the endometrium, causing periodic bleeding beyond the natural menopause. This, plus the possible side-effects of breast tenderness, swelling and secretion, make HRT unacceptable to many women. Hysterectomy eliminates the need for the addition of progestogens and eliminates their side-effects.

The question of the development of breast cancer with hormone therapy is now regarded more seriously than ever, and caution is advised—careful medical monitoring throughout treatment is necessary.

Prevention of osteoporosis is of paramount importance. Aiming at healthy bones in adolescence is most desirable, with attention to a diet that includes vitamin C to help develop a healthy bony matrix for the laying down of the essential chemicals, and calcium-rich dairy products. The elimination of unhealthy practices such as excess alcohol and smoking will build good foundations for a life-style that will serve the woman well as she approaches the natural infertility of the menopause. While physical fitness through exercise is essential, excessive physical stress that causes delayed ovulation and infrequent menstruation should be avoided.

Research continues into the physiology of bone, and several agents are undergoing clinical trials. The results from the Women's Health Initiative and from numerous other studies indicate that HRT protects against osteoporosis. But in view of concerns about this therapy's propensity for increasing breast cancer risk, it is fortunate that there are alternative preventive strategies, including the bisphosphonates and raloxifene which may lower breast-cancer risk.[8]

The cervical mucus and your gynaecological health

Once you can recognise your normal mucus pattern, any significant deviation—such as blood-stained or profuse mucus—indicates the need for a medical examination.

Any unusual bleeding should also be investigated and a satisfactory explanation provided.

Natural irregular bleeding can be explained by knowing the mucus pattern. This can spare a woman unnecessary curettage. Early diagnosis of disorders offers the best prospect of a successful treatment.

If all examinations and investigations prove normal and you are not taking synthetic hormones (as explained, these confuse diagnosis by causing uterine bleeding and mucus changes), charting may indicate that the mucus pattern you are now observing signifies a new situation of infertility.

SYMBOLS CODE FOR CHARTS

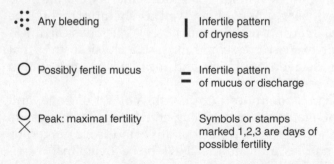

Any bleeding

Possibly fertile mucus

Peak: maximal fertility

Infertile pattern of dryness

Infertile pattern of mucus or discharge

Symbols or stamps marked 1,2,3 are days of possible fertility

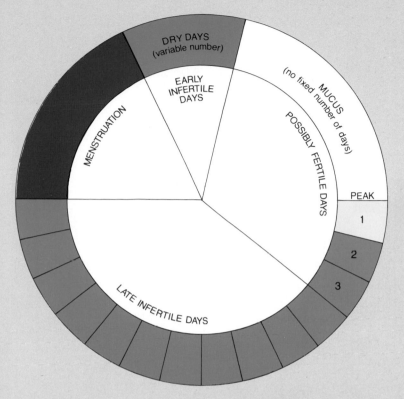

THE MENSTRUAL CYCLE
The mucus pattern of fertility and infertility

COLOUR CODE FOR CHARTS

Any bleeding

Infertile pattern
of dryness

Possibly
Fertile mucus

Infertile pattern
of mucus

Peak: maximal fertility

Stamps marked
1,2,3 are days of
possible fertility

Figure 1(a) First record of cycle

1	2	3	4	5	6	7	8	9	10	11	12	13	14	15	16	17	18	19	20	21	22	23	24	25	26	27	28	29

sticky cloudy wet · clear stretchy slippy wet wet · X · 1 2 3 · dry cloudy cloudy dry · dry cloudy shiny · wet · sticky cloudy cloudy wet wet

Figure 1(b) Same chart stamped for correct record of fertile and infertile mucus

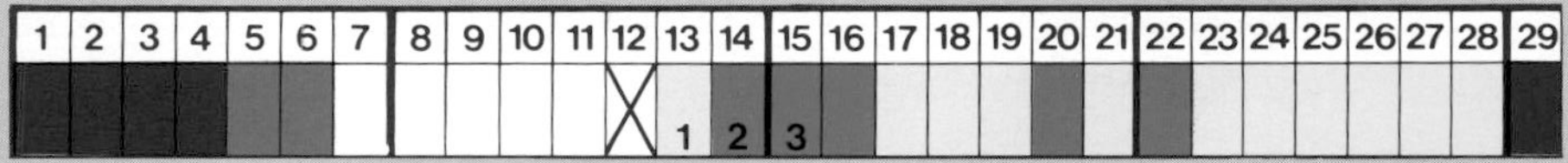

1	2	3	4	5	6	7	8	9	10	11	12	13	14	15	16	17	18	19	20	21	22	23	24	25	26	27	28	29

X · 1 2 3

Figure 1(c) Applying the guidelines to the cycle

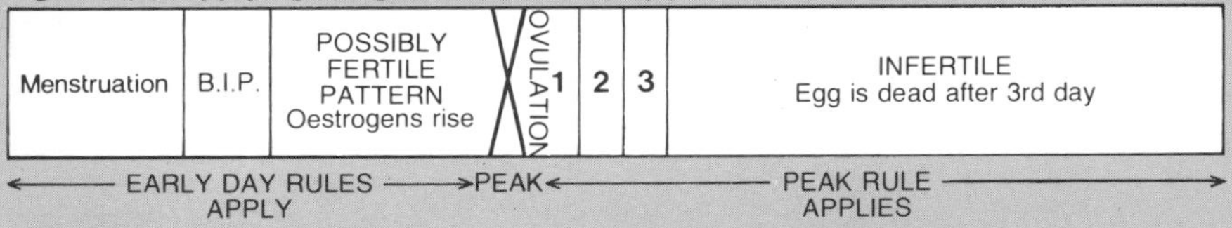

Menstruation	B.I.P.	POSSIBLY FERTILE PATTERN Oestrogens rise	OVULATION ✕ 1 2 3	INFERTILE Egg is dead after 3rd day

←— EARLY DAY RULES APPLY —→ · —→PEAK←— · —— PEAK RULE APPLIES ——

Figure 2 A short cycle

1	2	3	4	5	6	7	8	9	10	11	12	13	14	15	16	17	18	19	20

X · 1 2 3 · wet slippy stringy

Figure 3 A long cycle

1	2	3	4	5	6	7	8	9	10	11	12	13	14	15	16	17	18	19	20	21	22	23	24	25	26	27	28	29	30	31	32	33	34	35	36	37

sticky · cloudy · wet wet clear stringy slippy slippy dry slippy · X 1 · X 1 · 1 2 3

CHARTING:
SOME COMMON EXAMPLES

Figure 1(a) FIRST RECORD OF A CYCLE. Record what you see and feel: red – bleeding; green – dryness; white – any mucus. Try to identify the Peak (X).

Figure 1(b) Record with a yellow stamp, mucus after the Peak.

Figure 1(c) Refer to chapter 6 where the guidelines are explained.

Figure 2 A SHORT CYCLE with the Peak on Day 5. Intercourse should be avoided on all days of bleeding because ovulation may occur early.

Figure 3 A LONG CYCLE with the Peak on Day 23. Careful charting after the supposed Peak (Day 21) is necessary because occasionally fertile characteristics return (Day 23).

Figure 4 THE EFFECT OF INTERCOURSE ON THE MUCUS. Note the effect of seminal fluid on the day following intercourse, and application of the Early Day Rules (chapter 6). From three days past the Peak, all days are available for intercourse.

130

Figure 5 CONTINUOUS MUCUS. When mucus is continuous, several cycles may be necessary to identify the point of change from infertile to fertile mucus. In this cycle a change in sensation (Day 8) marked the start of the fertile phase.

Figure 6(a) and 6(b) TWO INFERTILE CYCLES. Hormone analysis confirmed ovulation (Day 14/15) in both cycles but intercourse at this time did not result in conception for either woman. No mucus occurred in 6(a) and in 6(b) mucus was present but lacked fertile characteristics.

Figure 7 PREGNANCY ACHIEVED. The use of alternate days for intercourse enabled this couple to recognise the beginning of the fertile phase. (This is important if mucus is sparse.) The couple then used several days for intercourse to achieve a pregnancy.

Figure 8 A STRESS CYCLE. Stress on Day 9 alerted this woman to the possibility that ovulation might be delayed. The couple applied the Early Day Rules for the whole cycle because no clear Peak was recorded.

Figure 4 The effect of intercourse on the mucus

Figure 5 Continuous mucus

Figure 6(a) An infertile cycle

Figure 6(b) An infertile cycle

Figure 7 Pregnancy achieved

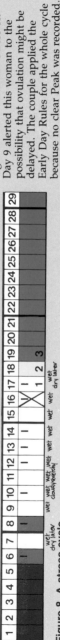

Figure 8 A stress cycle

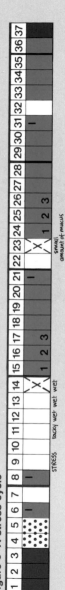

132

Figure 9 Cycles showing return to fertility after the Pill

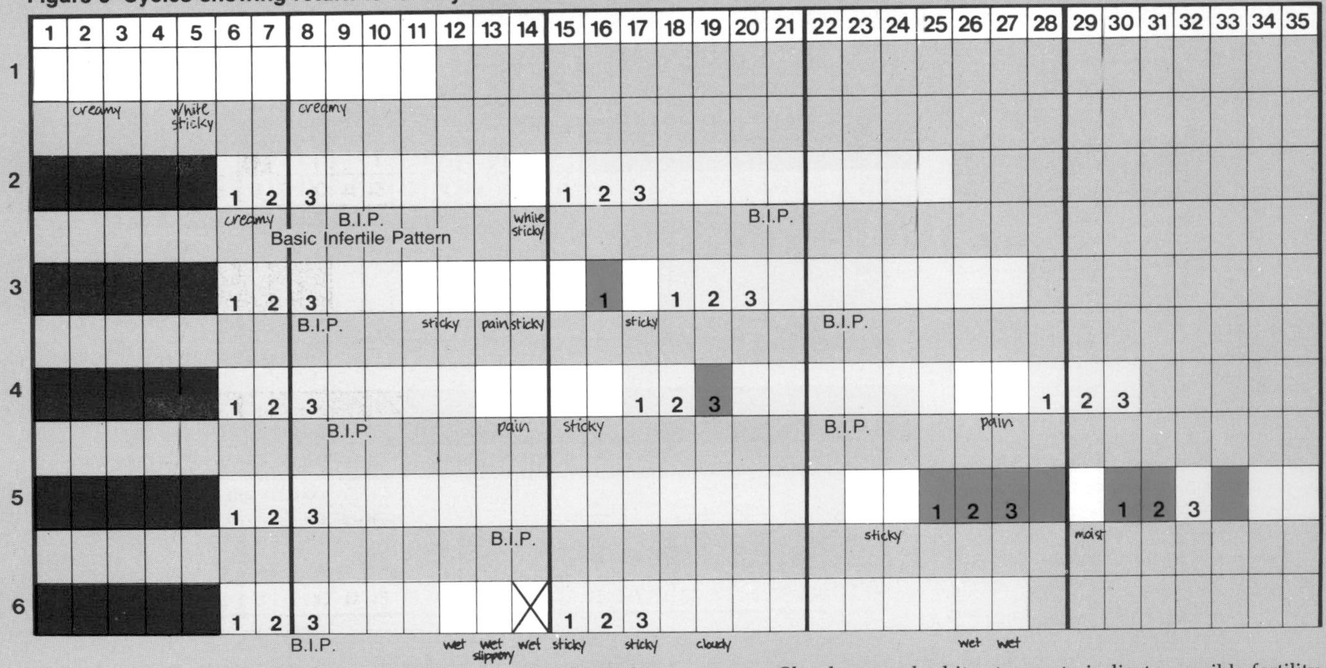

Figure 9 AFTER COMING OFF THE PILL. In her first learning chart, this woman recorded her observations of mucus with white stamps. After her first bleed she could recognise her Basic Infertile Pattern of mucus (see chapter 6) and marked these days with yellow stamps. She then used white stamps to indicate possible fertility when any change in the mucus was apparent. She ovulated in the last cycle. The count of 3 is not observed after true menstruation which always follows ovulation.

133

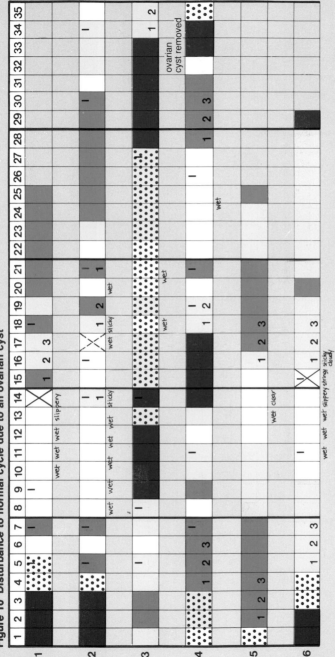

Figure 10 Disturbance to normal cycle to an ovarian cyst

Figure 10 AN ABNORMAL CYCLE — an ovarian cyst. The first line shows this woman's normal pattern. Then a long cycle occurred (lines 2 to 4), complicated by blood-spotting, an abnormal mucus pattern, and bleeding that she recognised as different from her normal menstrual flow. Such a change from her normal cycle alerted this woman to seek medical advice. An ovarian cyst was diagnosed and then removed (line 4). The pattern improved immediately, yet no Peak was recognised in the next cycle. Although a possibly fertile pattern was recorded in the last cycle, the return of fertility was delayed until the following cycle when pregnancy was achieved as desired.

Figure 11 Breastfeeding

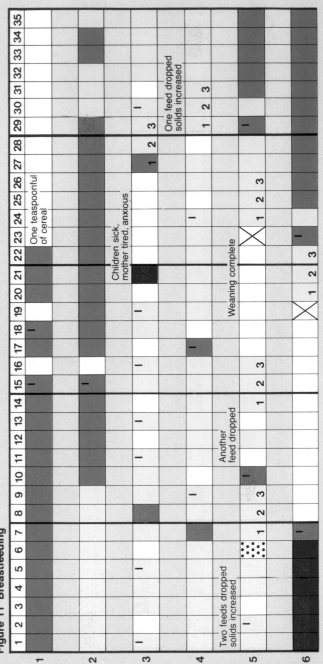

Figure 11 BREASTFEEDING. This is the chart of a woman who learned the method while breastfeeding her three-month-old baby. Two weeks charting without intercourse was sufficient to determine a continuing pattern of dryness (green stamp). Mucus with unchanging characteristics was recorded with a yellow stamp. All days following intercourse were recorded with a white stamp.

When the pattern changed (line 3) with bleeding and five days of fertile-type mucus, intercourse was deferred until three days after the return of the Basic Infertile Pattern. The Peak was recognised (line 5), indicating the return of fertility. (See chapter 10 for the method guidelines during breastfeeding.)

Figure 12 Approaching the menopause

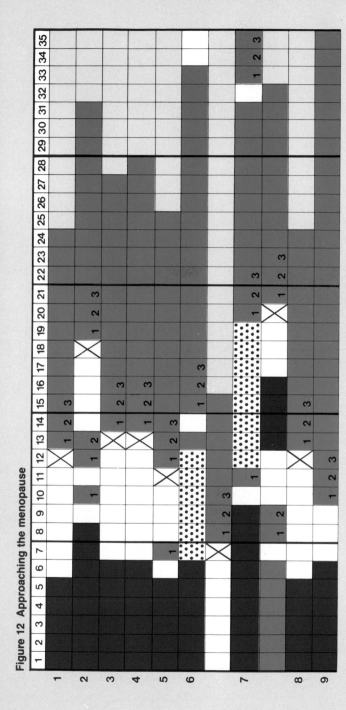

Figure 12 APPROACHING THE MENOPAUSE. When approaching the menopause a woman's normal pattern changes, leading to eventual infertility. This woman experienced irregularity, prolonged menstrual bleeding (cycles 6 and 7), a short interval between the

Peak and menstruation (cycle 6) and pre-ovulatory bleeding (cycle 7). By following the method guidelines outlined in chapters 6 and 11, this woman was able to assess her infertile and possibly fertile days. Following cycle 9 she recognised continuing infertility.

135

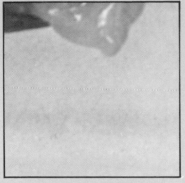

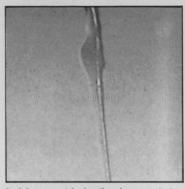

1. Pre-ovulatory mucus will not stretch, and breaks

2. Mucus with fertile characteristics prior to the Peak

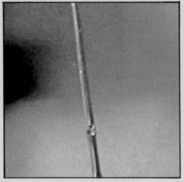

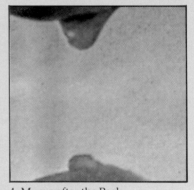

3. Mucus with fertile characteristics one or two days before the Peak *

4. Mucus after the Peak

THE KEY TO FERTILITY CONTROL: THE MUCUS

The photographs above show examples of one woman's mucus. Your own mucus may not look quite like this but you will quickly come to recognise what is fertile and what is infertile.

The mucus and the guidelines for the method are described in chapters 4, 5 and 6.

* While visual observations are valuable, due attention must be paid to the *sensation* the mucus produces. High fertility is signalled by the lubricative sensation which may persist a day or two after the mucus loses its stretchy appearance.

'For the past five years—since I was forty-three—my menstrual cycles have been irregular. At the beginning of this time I was using the Temperature Method.

The length of my cycles was sometimes sixty days, and in some cases there was no temperature rise, indicating that I was not always ovulating.

When ovulation did occur, I was using the post-ovulatory days for intercourse as well as the days of my menstrual bleeding.

My last child—now aged two—resulted from intercourse on the first day of bleeding after a long cycle; the bleeding was in fact associated with ovulation rather than the start of my menstrual period.

After the birth of this child, my husband and I were advised to abstain from intercourse for six months. We were told that if no menstrual period occurred during that time, I could assume that I was permanently infertile. Surely there was a better way. I then consulted an obstetrician who prescribed Norethisterone—a synthetic form of the hormone progesterone. The aim of this medication was to produce cycles of a regular length, so that I could use the Rhythm Method with temperature as a guide to fertile cycles. However, I did not bleed for six months, and then experienced a series of very heavy losses. I next developed headaches, pain in my arms and legs, and naturally enough, considerable anxiety. Everything was going wrong—including my marriage.

At this time, I heard about the Billings Method. Although sceptical, I sought the advice of a local Billings Method teacher.

My first chart after stopping Norethisterone indicated a Basic Infertile Pattern of unchanging, sticky mucus. It was not difficult to convince me to follow the Early Day Rule (intercourse on alternate nights) while the Basic Infertile Pattern continued. After a few patches of fertile-type mucus, my pattern settled down to a constant infertile pattern, and I knew that I could safely put all worries about a pregnancy behind me.'

Every woman must make decisions about how to manage her fertility as the menopause approaches. For some readers, the menopause is imminent; for others, it will occur some time in the future. Whatever your age, you will benefit from learning your signs of fertility and infertility now. It is not difficult to learn the method even when you are mostly infertile.

If you are in a dilemma—not knowing when to stop the Pill, or if you think sterilisation is the only way—don't despair. Remember, after two to four weeks of charting, most women can recognise the days when intercourse will not result in pregnancy.

The passage from fertility to infertility, when fully understood, is not difficult to negotiate. Symptoms which are not understood can be alarming and upsetting. Fertility regulation following the Billings Method is not difficult and removes much of the anxiety at this stage of a woman's reproductive life, and preserves and improves the bond between husband and wife. By maintaining the woman's health, early signs of disorders can be dealt with expeditiously and effectively. The knowledge that no harmful medication is necessary reassures the couple. Troublesome symptoms have other remedies and they will pass. A whole new life opens up for both.

CHAPTER 12

Difficulties in conceiving

It is estimated that approximately 20 per cent of couples trying to have a child are unable to do so. Yet most couples are unprepared for infertility and unaware that in many cases it can be overcome.

Infertility may produce many unexpected feelings—isolation, helplessness, guilt, anger, despair, and grief for the child not born. It may be the cause of mutual accusations, and create demands on partners, family, and friends, whose support and advice are sought.

However, the advice given is not always accurate or sympathetic. And unless it is scientifically well founded, suggestions about how to overcome an infertility problem can further damage an already disturbed relationship. So it is important to seek out doctors or counsellors who are knowledgeable in this field.

Infertility is usually defined as the inability to conceive after twelve to eighteen months of sexual intercourse without contraception.

The ability to conceive and give birth reaches its peak at about the age of twenty-five in both men and women. In women, reproductive ability declines between thirty and forty, then rapidly as the menopause approaches.

In men fertility gradually diminishes from about the age of fifty, or even earlier.

Many couples wanting a child who seek the help of a doctor will eventually conceive and give birth. They may have become unnecessarily alarmed at the delay in achieving a pregnancy. In many cases all that is needed is reassurance, provided by discussing the processes involved in reproduction and emphasising that intercourse without contraception does not guarantee an immediate pregnancy. Studies indicate that in those trying to conceive, fewer than a third will achieve their goal within the first month, only 50 per cent by six months, and 80 to 90 per cent by eighteen months.

Advice about timing intercourse to coincide with ovulation often proves invaluable. Some women produce mucus with fertile characteristics, essential if sperm are to reach the egg and maintain their fertilising capacity for only a day or two around the time of ovulation and only in some cycles. The Billings Method enables you to recognise this time of fertility and maximise your chances of conception occurring. It is advisable to use the Early Day Rules in order to identify the beginning of the fertile phase, and to ensure maximum sperm vitality. Then postpone intercourse until you recognise slippery mucus, which provides the maximum chance of conception. This simple information has helped many couples to conceive.

A temperature rise will provide confirmatory evidence of ovulation. However, it will be of no use in helping you time intercourse to coincide with ovulation since it usually occurs one to two days after ovulation (range four days before to six days after ovulation) by which time the egg is dead.

Causes of infertility

Infertility may be a temporary or a permanent problem, and should be viewed as the problem of a couple rather than of an individual even when the major component of the problem rests with one partner. Various studies indicate that in about one-third of cases, male factors are mainly responsible; and the main problem lies with the female partner in about another one-third of cases.

In the remainder, no cause of the infertility can be found, and contributory factors from both partners may be involved. Although the chances of achieving a pregnancy when the cause of infertility is unknown are often quoted as only 20 per cent, skilful counselling can increase the success rate substantially.

As new techniques of assessing infertility become available, and as we improve our understanding of the psychological, as well as the physical aspects of the problem, success rates are improving. The success of the various treatments depends on the age of the woman and to a lesser extent on the age of her partner, with older couples less likely to achieve a pregnancy. For women the supply of eggs, fixed at birth, is a limiting factor on pregnancy. So too is the quality of eggs, which deteriorates with age. The likelihood of having a child is further reduced in older women because natural pregnancy loss rates increase with age. Notwithstanding these facts, older couples of reproductive age are more likely to achieve parenthood if they stop smoking and reduce their weights to levels appropriate for their height and age.[1]

In this chapter we shall concentrate on some of the common causes of sub-fertility and infertility that can be helped by an awareness of the mucus. With many causes, the cervical mucus provides the first indication that all is not well. When treatment is successful, the mucus again acts as a signal—this time indicating the return of fertility.

The Billings Method and infertility

The clinical and experimental studies on the cervical mucus that provide the basis of the Billings Method have proved invaluable in the treatment of infertility.

Recognition of slippery mucus, coupled with the correct timing of intercourse to coincide with the Peak, have proved to be important factors in the improved management of infertility in recent years.

When you know that ovulation is imminent by observing your mucus signals, you have the knowledge to greatly increase your chances of conception. (See p. 43 for a description of the mucus signs.)

In some couples, suitable conditions for achieving a pregnancy—including the presence of mucus capable of supporting and assisting transport of the sperm cells—occur in only a few cycles each year, and perhaps for half a day only in each cycle. If you are having difficulty conceiving, you will need to be particularly watchful for these occasions.

'At first I thought I wasn't producing any mucus. Then, one day, after keeping watch for six months, I saw it. There was no doubt in my mind. We used that day for intercourse. The next day the fertile mucus was gone. Six weeks later doctors confirmed that our baby was on the way.'

But no amount of Billings Method knowledge can restore function to obstructed Fallopian tubes or remove cysts from ovaries, or rectify damage to the testes that is affecting sperm production. The Billings Method is not the answer to every infertility problem, and it would be quite wrong to delay a full medical investigation due to an exaggerated idea of what can be achieved by using the method. Once an underlying physical problem, such as blocked tubes, is rectified, the Billings Method can be used to advantage.

Increasingly, doctors who deal with infertility problems are recognising the value of the mucus signals, and are referring couples for skilled Billings Method tuition while they proceed with their independent investigations.

Competent teaching, backed by encouragement and the opportunity to discuss the mucus signals and their relationship to reproduction, is vital.

The importance of correct information

Incorrect information can contribute to apparent infertility. Some women, unaware of the significance of the fertile mucus, have believed it to be a sign of infection which could be transmitted to their partner. As a result, they have avoided intercourse at this, their most fertile time.

Others have been embarrassed by the profusion of the fertile-type mucus and, not recognising its importance, have likewise deferred intercourse. Attempts to remove it with douches and creams may have rendered the environment of the vagina hostile to sperm, contributing to an infertility problem.

Some couples try complicated and unnecessary techniques to achieve a pregnancy. They may, for example, have intercourse daily, which can prove counterproductive. For while some men can maintain a high quality of semen production with frequent—even daily—intercourse, others cannot.

Where frequent intercourse has occurred during the fertile phase of the cycle without a pregnancy resulting, it is likely that a rest from intercourse for a few days before the most fertile mucus appears will prove beneficial.

Factors involved in conception

The achievement of a pregnancy involves a complex chain of events. The egg cell must be healthy and must find its way from the ovary into the Fallopian tube. Healthy sperm cells must arrive in the vagina at a time when the cervical mucus is able to nourish and channel them through the uterus. The sperm passage along the Fallopian tube, assisted by the muscular movements of the uterus and tubes, must not be obstructed. Once fertilisation has occurred, the developing embryo must travel back through the tube to the uterus, arriving when both it, and the uterine lining, are at a suitable stage of development for implantation.

Precise timing and optimal conditions are crucial in a number of these events. And the disturbance of any one of the delicate physiological processes may make pregnancy difficult or even impossible to achieve. Many influences can tip the balance, including correct information and psychological factors.

During initial investigations, it usually becomes clear whether the basic problem is physical or psychological and, if the latter, whether time and reassurance will help.

Psychological factors: anxiety, tension

The investigation and management of infertility can itself stress couples, and it is not surprising that this can increase anxiety, which in turn can affect fertility.

Couples seeking help may be shy and anxious. The virility of the man and the femininity of the woman may seem to be in question, and investigations may loom large and threatening.

The fact that pregnancy often occurs when stress is taken out of the situation indicates how important psychological factors can be. An indication of their importance is the finding that 30 per cent of women undergoing artificial insemination fail to ovulate, or ovulate poorly during the stresses of the treatment period, after previously ovulating normally.

'After trying to have a child for six years without success, my husband and I decided to adopt a baby. Within six months I was pregnant. We can only conclude that our anxiety about conceiving somehow obstructed the normal course of events.'

Fatigue is sometimes a contributory factor to fertility problems. And a rest from work may provide the 'cure'. Undue stress from overwork or emotional distress is associated with lowered fertility in both men and women.

When the problem of infertility becomes an overriding concern, it is not uncommon for a woman to feel she is regarded as a producer rather than as a woman loved just for herself. It is a mistake to assume that 'everything will be all right if we can have a child.' When partners become totally important to each other 'no matter what', conception may happen unexpectedly—as though the baby had been waiting.

'Things were getting really bad. I had so many tests and so had Phil. I had kept a chart for eight months and everybody said we were normal . . . The best thing you told me after teaching me about the mucus was to forget the chart and concentrate on our life together. I gave up work, took some cooking lessons, pampered us both a bit and it happened. I really knew I was fertile. When I relaxed so did our love-making—and it became natural, not an exercise.'

Sometimes apparent infertility occurs when communication between partners breaks down. This may be reflected in a nervous sensitivity when one touches the other. This tension may prove a barrier to conception.

In such cases as this, conscious efforts by both partners to show a loving and caring attitude without looking for sexual rewards can help greatly.

Psychological factors can operate to produce a painful spasm of the vagina called vaginismus, or an inhibition of the secretions that normally lubricate the vagina. Both these conditions make intercourse difficult and emotionally distressing for both partners, and this may affect fertility.

Even normal functioning of the Fallopian tubes may be disturbed by anxiety.

On the male side, psychological influences can contribute to impotence, where an erection cannot be maintained adequately to allow successful vaginal penetration leading to orgasm and ejaculation. Highly specialised counselling may be warranted.

When both partners are involved in seeking a solution, lasting benefits are more likely. And when good information is available, couples themselves make the best counsellors. In the event where the problem of infertility cannot be overcome, working through the situation together often produces a strengthening of a relationship and an unbreakable bond of mutual love and support.

Investigations

Early investigation of infertility should involve both partners. It should include:
- A medical history of both partners including sexual development, past contraceptive usage, tuberculosis or pelvic inflammatory disease, stress situations, excessive tiredness, weight problems, and venereal disease.
- Charting the menstrual cycle according to the Billings Method. The cervical mucus pattern will provide information about some of the essentials of fertility. It also provides information about a woman's gynaecological health which may help unravel the infertility problem. For instance, disturbance of the mucus pattern may suggest the presence of infection, ovarian cysts, endometriosis or other abnormalities, particularly of the cervix. A hormonal disturbance may be

---

INSTRUCTIONS FOR ACHIEVING PREGNANCY

Following menstruation, intercourse is available on alternate evenings during dryness or unchanging discharge (BIP).

When a change from the BIP occurs, wait without genital contact until slippery mucus develops. Concentrate intercourse on days of slipperiness and for a day or two after the discharge changes. (See page 37.)

N.B. Some women achieve pregnancy without ever having seen any mucus. The unmistakable change in sensation from dry to slippery is the key to recognising fertility, and intercourse on this day has proved to be most successful.

It is a comfort for a couple to know accurately the expected delivery date of their baby. It is misleading to calculate the delivery date from the last menstruation, which bears no relation to the time of the following ovulation when conception occurs. It could be weeks or months later. This valuable information helps ensure that there is no interference with a normal pregnancy and helps allow the baby to go to term before birth. The expected delivery date is 266 days + or – 6 days from the Peak.

---

suspected in the absence of fertile mucus and will require investigation.

• Physical examination of both partners including a complete gynaecological examination of the woman.

Further investigations may include an assessment of hormone levels, a Huhner's (post-coital) test, a hysterosalpingogram, laparoscopy and ultrasound.

HORMONE ASSESSMENT   Identifying the mucus signs of fertility, the medical history and physical examination are

the most important elements in the assessment of reproductive dysfunction. Laboratory tests are generally used
only to confirm what is suspected from a specialist's
initial evaluation.[2] The procedure followed depends on
the symptoms of the fertility problem. In the absence of a
recognisable mucus pattern, the hormones from the
ovaries are studied. These and further investigations
require the attention of a specialist.

A number of women who are unsuccessful in becoming
pregnant have a very poor mucus secretion accompanying ovulation. Some of these women will conceive if they
are taught to recognise the mucus by paying attention
to the sensation that a very small amount of mucus
produces at the vulva, without any being visible. Sometimes a woman will ovulate regularly but produce mucus
only sometimes.

Luteal phases (the intervals between ovulation and
menstruation) which are short, or are deficient in
hormones, are often seen in the cycles of women coming
off contraceptive medication, but also may be due to
imperfect ovulation in immaturity, approaching the
menopause, and at any time for no known reason. These
conditions can be corrected by suitable medication given
in the pre-ovulatory phase of the cycle in order to enhance a weak ovulation. The Ovarian Meter has proved
to be of great assistance in guiding the woman to the
precise time of ovulation and confirming her slight observations (see p. 215). Considerable success has resulted. By
being able to determine the onset of the oestrogen rise
and the beginning of the fertile phase as well as defining
ovulation, both the Billings Method and the Ovarian
Meter have the advantage of defining infertility ahead of
ovulation, thus giving the couple freedom for intercourse
with security, no matter how short or long the pre-
ovulatory phase.

After the baby is born it is essential for the woman to be

sure of her infertility until she approaches ovulation again, maybe months later.

Professor Eric Odeblad recognised that a post-Pill infertility was caused by shrinkage of the crypts in the upper cervical canal that normally produce fertile mucus.[3] This problem has now been identified in many countries. While some of these women will eventually conceive after nature has been allowed to heal the cervix over two years or more, some women will never conceive. The effect of the Pill on fertility has caused much anguish among couples in the thirties age group who voluntarily delayed pregnancy for personal reasons, because they were not warned of this problem.

The Ovarian Meter monitors the return of the normal hormonal ovulatory pattern.

HUHNER'S TEST (POST-COITAL TEST)   This test involves the collection of a mucus sample from the cervix about four to twelve hours after intercourse around the time of your Peak fertility, as judged by the mucus. A semen analysis is made by studying the number, activity and form of sperm cells under high magnification.

The value of the Huhner's test is that it assesses the compatibility of your partner's sperm with your mucus with fertile characteristics, and confirms that intercourse has successfully deposited sperm cells in the vagina.

The test must be timed to coincide with the fertile mucus near or at the Peak of fertility, since the sperm cells die promptly in an unfavourable mucus environment.

The Huhner's test may indicate compatible sperm–mucus interaction, or it may suggest disorders of sperm production, cervical or vaginal infections, hostile mucus at the time of ovulation, or—very rarely—the presence of sperm antibodies which destroy or damage the sperm.

HYSTEROSALPINGOGRAM   A hysterosalpingogram involves taking X-ray pictures of the reproductive organs while a radiopaque dye is injected through the vagina into the Fallopian tubes. This helps to determine whether the tubes are closed off, for example by scar tissue or following an inflammation which has caused the tubal lining to adhere in places.

The hysterosalpingogram shows the shape of the uterine cavity, the state of each tube, and the site of an obstruction, if any. Such obstruction may be suspected following any pelvic or abdominal infection.

Sometimes, performing a hysterosalpingogram will clear the Fallopian tubes of minor obstruction and a pregnancy may follow soon afterwards.

LAPAROSCOPY   Doctors may use the technique of laparoscopy or culdoscopy to check that the Fallopian tubes are open and to investigate physical abnormalities such as ovarian cysts, endometriosis, fibroids of the uterus, or tubal adhesions which may be affecting your fertility. These procedures involve introducing a telescope-like instrument either through the abdominal wall or the vaginal wall to directly observe the internal organs. A dye may also be introduced during laparoscopy to enable assessment of the internal organs.

ULTRASOUND TECHNOLOGY   Ultrasound technology has achieved high levels of accuracy in capable hands. A non-invasive procedure used to study abnormalities of internal organs, this technique has been of special value in obstetrics and gynaecology particularly when used in conjunction with the Billings Method charting and hormonal monitoring.

Physical causes of infertility

Important advances have been made in this area in recent times.

In a significant proportion of infertile couples, the reasons for infertility remain obscure. A review of twenty-one published studies involving assessments of 14 141 infertile couples concluded that ovulatory disorders accounted for infertility in 27 per cent of cases, abnormal sperm counts and associated abnormalities for 25 per cent, defects of the Fallopian tubes for 22 per cent, endometriosis 5 per cent, a variety of other causes 4 per cent, leaving 17 per cent of cases unexplained.[4]

Looking specifically at women with infertility problems, the World Health Organisation (WHO) Taskforce on Diagnosis and Treatment of Infertility concluded that ovulatory disorders and tubal abnormalities are often implicated (involved in 25 per cent and 22 per cent of cases respectively). Other conditions identified in female infertility are endometriosis (15 per cent), pelvic adhesions (12 per cent) and hormonal conditions (7 per cent), the latter including excessive production of the hormone prolactin, which stimulates breast milk production. In 15–20 per cent of women with infertility no abnormality can be identified.[5]

Problems associated with the ovaries and ovulation

Disorders associated with the ovaries may be suggested by abnormalities of the mucus pattern, or by disturbance of the normal menstrual pattern. An imperfect ovulation may result in a shorter than normal luteal phase (the interval between ovulation and menstruation). Low hormone levels, a short luteal phase, or failure of the follicle to release the egg, all indicate infertility.

Failure to release egg cells may be due to a fault within the ovaries themselves, or to failure of one or both of the hormones released by the pituitary gland (Follicle Stimulating Hormone and Luteinising Hormone). Urine analysis of hormones can readily furnish information about ovulation. Blood tests are also available.

These hormones in their turn may be deficient due to

lack of a 'releasing hormone' from the hypothalamus which triggers their output.

Rarely, the ovaries 'dry-up' prematurely and no egg cells are available. No fertile mucus is produced. This happens to every woman in the months or years before the menopause. But every now and then it occurs much earlier and is then called premature ovarian failure.

Some women have regular monthly periods but do not ovulate: these are termed 'anovulatory bleeds'. On keeping a daily mucus record it is seen that there is no Peak. Hormonal investigations show a persistently low production of the hormone progesterone throughout the menstrual cycle, and the absence of a rise in basal body temperature indicates that ovulation has not occurred.

Other women will notice that they have fertile mucus only occasionally, and their cycles may be very irregular. Medical investigation is necessary to determine whether lack of fertile mucus in most cycles is due to a failure to ovulate or an abnormality of the cervix. Treatment with fertility drugs to induce ovulation often proves successful (see p. 155).

Some women who are seeking help for failure to conceive find, when taught to keep a mucus record, that although they are ovulating and cycling regularly they cannot observe visually or by sensation any changes at the vulva. Hormonal monitoring sometimes shows a sustained high progesterone level in the pre-ovulatory phase which is responsible for the suppression of mucus and consequent infertility. Progesterone rises even further after ovulation, maintaining an abnormally high level until menstruation is imminent. This condition, referred to as the adreno-genital syndrome, is due to an enzyme deficiency (21 Alpha Hydroxylase) in the adrenal gland, which can be treated by Dexamethasone. Normal progesterone levels are restored, cervical mucus is produced and pregnancy is usually achieved.

Sometimes menstruation fails to occur (a condition known as amenorrhoea) and except where the uterus is abnormal, this means that ovulation has failed. Amenorrhoea is defined as the absence of menstruation for six months or more. Stress, fatigue, psychological disturbances, obesity, weight loss, anorexia nervosa, thyroid disease, diabetes, an abnormal growth of the pituitary gland, or the Pill, are among the causes.

A significant number of women with absent or infrequent bleeding of less than one year's duration, or with amenorrhoea after coming off the Pill, ovulate spontaneously during the investigation period. This may be due to reassurance provided by sympathetic and well-informed counsellors and doctors.

Another possible cause of amenorrhoea is an excess of the hormone prolactin produced by the pituitary gland in the brain. (Prolactin is the hormone which stimulates breast milk production.) This situation requires skilful medical management to exclude the possibility of a tumour of the pituitary gland. Any young woman whose cycles have recently altered in mucus pattern or bleeding frequency should be investigated for the possibility of an abnormally high prolactin level. She should be asked specifically whether she has noticed any secretion from the nipples or whether she is able to express any milk. The drug Cabergoline is often used in managing excessive prolactin production, with Bromocriptine as another option.

A common cause of sub-fertility related to the ovaries is polycystic ovary syndrome (PCOS). This occurs when both ovaries are enlarged by multiple cysts, resulting in a disturbed mucus pattern and intermittent bleeding. In the case of PCOS, secretion of the Follicle Stimulating Hormone may be below normal levels, while that of the Luteinising Hormone is elevated. The latter may result in excessive hair production, severe acne, obesity, irregular menstruations due to infrequent ovulation, and lowered fertility.

PCOS is associated with insulin resistance and consequent raised levels of insulin and fat in the blood;[6] tests for diabetes should be performed. Metformin is often effective for both diabetes and PCOS: it can restore ovulation and normal cycle length; it is also beneficial in treating acne and hairiness. Metformin enhances the action of Clomid in stimulating ovulation and achieving pregnancy. [7,8]

DIAGNOSIS AND TREATMENT   Through various tests, your doctor will assess at which level the problem lies. These tests may include hormonal analysis of blood or urine samples.

Tubal abnormalities

This is one of the most common identifiable causes of infertility, and is often difficult to correct.

The Fallopian tubes are particularly vulnerable to infection, and any scarring or destruction of the delicate tube lining may affect the passage of sperm or egg, making conception impossible. If the microscopic hairs lining the tubes—so vital to sperm and egg movement—are damaged, this may disrupt the synchronisation necessary for implantation of the developing embryo in the nutritive endometrium. In humans this mutual suitability of uterus and the embryo exists for only about thirty-six hours.

Likewise, the muscular lining of the tubes which is partially responsible for sperm and egg movement must be in good condition. If movement along the tube is too slow, the embryo may implant and develop within the tube, resulting in an ectopic pregnancy. This carries an increased risk of rupture and destruction of the tube, loss of the embryo, and reduced fertility (since only one Fallopian tube will then be functioning). Or if movement along the tube is too fast, the embryo can be hurried into the uterus before the imbedding site is ready to accept it. Hormones control this time-sensitive mechanism and synthetic hormones can disrupt it.

DIAGNOSIS AND TREATMENT   What if both partners are in good health and charting of the mucus indicates a normal pattern, yet conception fails to occur after intercourse during the fertile phase of two to three cycles? The next step is to do a Huhner's (post-coital) test and to check the Fallopian tubes are not blocked by performing a hysterosalpingogram, laparoscopy, and/or ultrasound.

A medical history may suggest how damage to the delicate hair-lined channel or muscle walls of the tubes has occurred. Possible causes include infections, surgery, a ruptured appendix, tuberculosis, venereal disease, especially gonorrhoea and chlamydia, as well as other pelvic infections.[9]

Adhesions—bands of fibrous tissue which may develop following inflammation, endometriosis or surgery—may require surgical removal. The success of the treatment varies according to the extent of the damage, especially if the fringed ends of the tubes near the ovary (the fimbriae) are involved.

If the cause of the infertility is a previous sterilisation involving burning or tying of the tubes, and a reversal is now sought, this may be possible; however, only limited success has been achieved to date.

Fertility drugs

In assessing ovarian hormonal disorders, a short or hormonally deficient luteal phase may be diagnosed. This is amenable to correction by the appropriate fertility drug.

CLOMIPHENE (CLOMID)   This is a synthetic anti-oestrogen which appears to induce ovulation by stimulating the release of the Follicle Stimulating Hormone (FSH) and Luteinising Hormone (LH). It is often used for women who wish to have a baby and whose ovulatory mechanism is inadequate. Ovulation does not always follow on day 14 after giving Clomid, as is often supposed, but may be as late as day 21 or later. A mucus record should be kept to detect the fertile phase and the Peak of fertility. If ovulation does occur soon after Clomid is given, the mucus may be very poor. However, if ovulation is delayed the raised oestrogen level will increase mucus production.

Considerable success in achieving conception has followed the administration of Clomid in 25 mg doses daily for five days following menstruation. If unsuccessful, the treatment is repeated in the next cycle, and again at a later date, raising the dose to 50 mg. If unsuccessful, the treatment could be repeated after several months.

GONADOTROPHINS   The most potent and expensive fertility drugs available, these include Human Chorionic Gondotrophin (HCG), Human Menopausal Gonadotrophin (HMG) and Human Pituitary Gonadotrophin (HPG). They bypass the hypothalamus and pituitary gland and substitute for the pituitary hormones, FSH and LH.

The effectiveness of Gonadotrophins depends on whether the ovaries are capable of being stimulated. Cases have been reported of ovaries dormant for many years responding with full ovulation within ten days of commencing therapy. Close supervision is essential, since overstimulation of the ovaries can easily occur, resulting in the rapid development of large ovarian cysts, or in multiple births.

A high ovulation rate of 90 per cent can be achieved under careful supervision. Sixty per cent or more of women treated become pregnant. And 20 per cent of such pregnancies are multiple births, mainly twins.

If the problem is a short post-ovulatory phase of eleven

days or less (as can be readily seen by charting the mucus pattern), HCG helps to prevent premature shedding of the endometrium by ensuring adequate ovulation and proper formation of the corpus luteum.

A poor mucus secretion can be greatly improved. By means of Gonadotrophins, oestrogen production is increased and this stimulates a more abundant mucus production by the cervix, the essential requirement for conception.

Infections

A woman's fertility may be impaired by pelvic inflammatory disease, which refers to infections of the reproductive organs, particularly those affecting the Fallopian tubes. The disease may follow procedures such as curettage or IUD insertion, or may be sexually transmitted.

An infection may or may not produce symptoms. Often damage is done before investigations detect the organism responsible. Early treatment is essential.

A multitude of factors may affect the internal environment. Douches, vaginal creams, and sometimes the use of the Pill create an environment suitable for the growth of certain organisms. One study showed that the risk of uterine infection in women under the age of thirty with IUDs is five times greater than among non-IUD users.[10] It is thought that the offending IUDs may cause a break in the endometrial surface, thus permitting bacterial invasion of the endometrium and of adjacent blood and lymph vessels.

A study co-ordinated by the World Health Organisation indicates that an IUD should never be inserted into any woman who may have been infected recently by organisms that cause sexually transmitted diseases, such as gonococci or chlamydia.[11] (See p. 184). Research suggests that the micro-organism T-mycoplasma is associated with pelvic inflammatory disease,[12] as is chlamydia. The IUD string acts as a wick along which infection travels into the uterus. Unwashed fingers feeling for the string to see that the IUD is still in place are responsible. An unpleasant odour, itching, soreness and burning when urinating indicate such an infection. Persistent back pain often follows, as pelvic inflammatory disease becomes established.

Chlamydia causes sterility by damage to the tubes and cervix, and often produces no vaginal discharge. Sexually transmitted, it must be treated early by antibiotics to prevent damage. These organisms are thought to disrupt implantation of the embryo, one of the factors responsible for infertility.

Douches and chemicals used in the vagina

Douches, vaginal deodorants, and lubricative jellies have been associated with diminished fertility. These preparations may contain chemicals capable of killing sperm cells, or they may disturb the vaginal environment by causing allergies or inflammatory reactions which impair sperm survival. They also tend to obscure the mucus pattern, making assessment of your fertile phase difficult. They should be discontinued to maximise the chances of a pregnancy occurring.

The damaged cervix

Before it was realised that the cervical mucus was essential for sperm survival, it was common practice to cauterise the cervix severely in order to dispose of the discharge that the woman presumed to be a disease. This, of course, destroyed her fertility.

It is now appreciated that the cervix deserves very

gentle treatment and surgical procedures, and those designed to treat infections, cancer, ulcerations and other abnormalities are used conservatively. Painting with silver nitrate, and treatment by diathermy (heat), cryo-surgery (cold) and laser beams, are among the options. Surgical coning may be necessary to eradicate a cancerous area.

An altered mucus pattern will be apparent after treatment and must be evaluated by careful observations. It is essential to pay attention to sensations at the vulva. The Ovarian Meter may be valuable in these circumstances.

Production by the cervix of abnormal mucus

Occasionally a thick, sticky mucus may be due to an infected cervix. When the offending organism is identified and treated, the fertile characteristics return and conception becomes possible.

Thick mucus results also from medication with progestogens, and when this medication is stopped, the mucus returns to normal with fertile characteristics, after some time. The use of ethinyl oestradiol to improve the mucus has not been successful in achieving pregnancy.

Endometriosis

Endometriosis is the growth of the endometrial tissue on the tubes, ovaries, urinary, or intestinal organs. The symptoms vary but women troubled by painful menstrual cramps or uncomfortable intercourse and prolonged menstrual bleeding should seek medical advice.

A woman who is familiar with her normal mucus pattern may detect this abnormality at an early stage by the disturbed pattern as well as by prolonged bleeding and spotting.

If endometriosis is identified as the cause of infertility,

treatment in the form of surgery or hormonal therapy may help. The surgical treatment is long and meticulous. The synthetic hormone Danazol is often used. It abolishes ovulation and therefore prevents menstrual bleeding, together with bleeding from all the other abnormal deposits of endometrial tissue, allowing them to shrink.

Doctors may advise women in whom the condition is not yet well advanced to have their families as soon as possible, because of the possibility that the abnormal growth will irreversibly block the Fallopian tubes. Hormonal treatment may contribute further to the infertility. In some cases, pregnancy itself has a beneficial effect on halting the endometriosis.

Smoking

A consistent and highly significant trend of decreasing fertility in women with an increasing number of cigarettes smoked per day has been reported.[13]

Smoking has been associated with an altered urinary oestrogenic profile during the menstrual cycle. In view of the changed mucus patterns attributable to smoking observed by Billings Method users, the infertility associated with heavy smoking may have a cervical explanation.

Many of the subjects in the study had stopped contraceptive medication in order to become pregnant. The effects of oral contraception are shown by Odeblad to have a profound effect on fertility by damage to the cervix. Gradual return to fertility can be monitored by the Billings Method, illustrating recovery of the normal fertile mucus pattern.

Smoking and the Pill have both been implicated in the development of cancer of the cervix.[14] More research is needed to clarify cervical damage in infertility due to smoking and contraceptive medication.

Male infertility

It is important to emphasise the distinction between fertility and the other major male characteristic of virility or potency. The majority of men who are infertile are normally virile.

Much remains to be learnt about the causes and treatment of male infertility, which usually involves a disruption of sperm production, maturation and/or transport. Known causes of male infertility include genetic factors; birth abnormalities; obstruction of the vas (the tube that carries the sperm from the testes to the penis); infections such as mumps after puberty, tuberculosis and venereal disease; chronic ill-health; and varicocele (an abnormality of the blood vessels of the testes). Rarely, the infertility results from a hormonal disturbance.

Acute feverish illnesses, emotional shock, and very frequent intercourse can also lower the sperm-count temporarily and this is one reason why too much attention should not be paid to a single sperm-count which is in the sub-fertile range.

Sperm counts fluctuate spontaneously and over a wide range. Any investigation of infertility in men should include:

- A full medical history and physical examination.
- A Huhner's (post-coital) test. This enables the quality of the semen to be assessed, and a sperm count to be made, and indicates how the sperm cells are behaving. The test must coincide with fertile mucus. Otherwise the sperm will quickly disappear.
- An assessment of psychological factors which may contribute to infertility, such as undue stress or fatigue. The Huhner's test is a more accurate guide to sperm health than a sperm count alone. For a sperm count gives no indication of whether the sperm are able to

survive in the female genital tract or of whether the technique of intercourse is effective.

Also, the 'normal range' of sperm in a whole ejaculate is 40 to 900 million. However, these counts are obtained from a masturbatory specimen which may vary greatly depending on anxiety, general health, or frequency of intercourse. Smoking is now thought to be one cause of defective sperm production.

The criteria for 'normal' sperm counts have sometimes been set far too high, and in some cases men told they are infertile, on the basis of a sperm count, later become fathers. A man should never be told he is infertile unless he is producing no sperm at all.

The relationship between infertility and sperm antibodies is not yet clear. However, even in women who produce these antibodies to their partner's sperm, pregnancy sometimes occurs. Treatment with cortisone has been helpful in some cases.

Treatment of male infertility is sometimes unsatisfactory because in more than a quarter of the cases, no cause can be found. Even when a cause is identified, the effectiveness of treatments is often controversial.[15] However there is growing optimism in this field of medicine as new techniques are developed to assist men with semen abnormalities to become parents.

Assisted reproductive technology (ART)

Since this book was first published, artificial insemination by sperm from a husband or donor, in-vitro fertilisation (IVF), gamete intra-Fallopian transfer (GIFT) and other variations on the IVF procedure have been developed and/or more fully assessed. Surrogate motherhood is finding little appeal. This is not to be wondered at as the vital mother–child relationship is severed and the pregnant woman may find it difficult to give up her baby at birth.

A major innovation in the treatment of male infertility in recent years has been intracytoplasmic sperm injection (ICSI). This has enabled the treatment of men with very low or even absent sperm counts, as sperm may be obtained from the testis for injection into the egg. In 2000, in Australia and New Zealand, ICSI with transfer of fresh or frozen embryos accounted for 51.4 per cent of all embryo transfers.[16]

Some assisted conception techniques involve artifical stimulation of multiple ovulations, with sperm being added to the collected eggs to allow fertilisation to take place. However, severe hyper-stimulation occurs at times, resulting in a life-threatening condition which requires extensive treatment and hospitalisation.[17] In 1999, 2.4 per cent of women taking part in assisted conception programs in Australia and New Zealand required hospitalisation for ovarian hyper-stimulation syndrome.[18]

If spare embryos are produced during ART procedures, they may be discarded, frozen or used for experimentation. Moves to limit the number of embryos selected for implantation have been successful in reducing the number of multiple pregnancies. This eliminates the practice of reduction abortion.

A major deficiency in the field of assisted reproduction is the lack of randomised studies demonstrating the superiority of the new techniques compared to other forms of fertility treatment. Another issue is the introduction of many techniques and technologies without a clinical trial to demonstrate their preferability over 'standard' methods of treatment. Many ART procedures are scientifically inefficient in achieving the birth of live, normal babies. In Victoria, which has a proven track record in establishing infertility treatment programs, in 1999 little more than half the eggs collected were successfully fertilised and only 4.2 per cent of the resulting embryos developed to be babies[19] (some estimates put this figure at closer to 3 per cent). Such a loss of embryonic life is morally unacceptable to many people, and the figures stand in contrast to the success rate of the Billings Method of natural conception, which is 80 per cent or higher depending on the couple's fertility. Nature has provided for natural fertilisation with the cervical mucus providing an excellent mechanism of selection, nutrition, and transplant of the best sperm. Such precision ensures the best environment for the health of the embryo and hence a very low risk of early death.

In a given year, about one in five women embarking on IVF in Victoria has a baby. In Australia and New Zealand overall, significant complications affect 15 per cent of pregnancies occurring after assisted reproduction.[20] The important point here is that these figures are about as good as it gets. Couples contemplating IVF should be aware that claimed success rates for IVF and other forms of assisted reproduction may be inflated by selecting for treatment only those individuals most likely to achieve pregnancy. It is therefore important that couples considering assisted reproduction carefully assess the clinical characteristics of the couples involved, such as the age of the female partner and the cause of infertility. Couples should also be aware that the results of treatment vary considerably from centre to centre.

Rates of spontaneous abortion tend to be high following assisted conception, with about one in five women experiencing a spontaneous abortion and up to one in 45 having an ectopic pregnancy. The stress and disappointment for parents in these circumstances are understandably great. The use of frozen and spare embryos remains very controversial, and distressing for those concerned for newly conceived human life. Legislators are attempting to ensure that scientists engaged in research and experimentation in this field do not devalue or leave unprotected young lives and parents.

Facing infertility

Although IVF was originally developed for women with severe tubal disease, the procedure is frequently offered to women with ill-defined infertility problems. It is not uncommon, when IVF fails, for proper Billings Method instruction to succeed. It is heartening to see the growing number of textbooks and articles on human reproduction referring in considerable detail to the importance of cervical mucus and its variations.[21, 22, 23] If tubal damage has sterilised the woman, the realisation may prove difficult to accept and extremely disheartening. However, if partners can think of this as something to face together, they may find that instead of separating them it brings them closer.

It sometimes happens that when partners have become resigned to childlessness and have developed a contentment with each other, a pregnancy unexpectedly occurs, confounding the cleverest doctors.

CHAPTER 13

The technological approach to contraception

While the Pill has been responsible for enabling many women to take effective control of their fertility, it has not been without a cost. The enthusiasm of the early 1960s has been tempered by increasing caution due to reports of complications of both short- and long-term use.

Health authorities advise women over the age of thirty-five who smoke to find an alternative method of fertility control. It is also advised that the Pill be prescribed with caution for women over the age of forty. There is a trend towards the use of condoms, sterilisation and abortion; but many women find these methods unsatisfactory or unacceptable.

Fertility control should be reliable, harmless, immediately reversible, and inexpensive. It should not detract from the pleasure of sexual intercourse and it should encourage a good emotional and sexual relationship between partners. How do the available artificial contraceptives measure up against these criteria?

Despite the large input of money and research into new methods in recent years, most methods fall down somewhere along the line. Indeed, couples seeking to limit or space their families face a real dilemma. Should they try alternating physical barrier methods—such as condoms or diaphragms—with the Pill or with natural methods? Should they rely on the Pill or the IUD and risk suffering their side-effects? Or does the finality of sterilisation hold the only solution? For each couple, this is a serious and individual decision. One of the most vital considerations is the effectiveness of the various methods.

In practice, every known method of fertility control has a failure rate, and these are discussed in this and the next chapter. Some methods have a significantly lower failure rate than others—for example the Pill is less prone to failure than, say, contraceptive foam. Yet there is a growing realisation that the method failure rate is not the only consideration. What are the side-effects? Are there aesthetic or moral objections? To what extent does success with a method depend on motivation?

It is the balancing of such factors that will finally help couples decide on a fertility control method that suits them.

Approaches to fertility control

To date the approaches to fertility control have included:
- Natural methods, where couples avoid intercourse during the fertile phase of the menstrual cycle and thus do not alter the body's natural processes. These methods are described in the next chapter.
- Sterilising methods, where the Fallopian tubes or vas deferens are divided, the uterus is removed or, in the case of types of Pill, where egg production is prevented.
- Contraceptive methods, where a physical or chemical barrier is placed between the sperm and the egg (e.g. with a diaphragm or condom, or a spermicidal cream), or where cervical mucus is rendered impenetrable.
- Abortive methods, where the embryo is prevented from continuing its normal development.

In this chapter, let us examine the safety and effectiveness of various artificial methods of fertility control.

Oral contraceptive pill

COMBINED PILL   Usually simply called the Pill, it is a combination of two synthetic hormones, oestrogen and progesterone. (Synthetic forms of progesterone are known as progestogens.)

The simplest form of combined pill is the Monophasic, in which all the hormone-containing pills are identical. Other types of Pill include the Biphasic and the Triphasic. The Biphasic (or two-step) Pill contains the same dose of oestrogen as in Monophasic pills, but the amount of progestogen rises to a higher dose after the first eleven pills. The net effect is less progestogen than in the Monophasic Pill. The Triphasic (or three-step) Pill is also designed to reduce the total amount of hormones taken during the month. The oestrogen content of tablets remains low except for a slight increase in mid-cycle, while the progestogen content increases in three stages during the cycle.

The vast majority of women using the Pill are prescribed formulations with low doses of hormones. In exceptional circumstances pills with higher dosages may be prescribed.

Triphasic pills have the advantages of having the lowest hormone dose of Combined Pill preparations, and fewer metabolic effects than other Combined Pills. Their disadvantages include the smaller margin for error (each tablet should be taken at roughly the same time each day) and therefore a possibly increased failure rate and increased blood loss compared with monophasics.

The high-dose Monophasic Pill is usually reserved for women who experience mid-cycle (breakthrough) bleeding when they take low-dose pills, are prone to excessive blood loss on other pills, are using medications that accelerate the breakdown of pill components (for example anti-epileptic drugs) or have become pregnant unexpectedly on a low-dose pill.

In the so-called 'third generation Pill', the oestrogen content has been further reduced, the progestogen level altered, and a greater variety of progestogens incorporated. It is only now, in the early years of the twenty-first century and a decade after the shift to third-generation Pills, that their impact on reproductive physiology is becoming apparent.

MINI PILL A single-hormone pill, containing only a progestogen, it must be taken every day at about the same time—or within at most three hours of the usual time—to be effective (compared with an allowable twelve-hour variation in the time of taking the regular Pill). Thus you are more likely to become pregnant than if you forget to take a regular Pill. The Mini Pill is often given to women who are breastfeeding.

How does the Pill work?

The regular Pill acts in a number of ways simultaneously. First it inhibits ovulation. The hormones in the Pill replace the normal production of oestrogen and progesterone by the ovaries. They suppress the triggering mechanism in the brain which causes the release of follicle stimulating hormone (FSH) and luteinising hormone (LH), and thus prevent ovulation in about 98 per cent of cycles.

Secondly, the progestogen component of the regular Pill stimulates the production of barrier (infertile-type) mucus. The aim here is to prevent sperm penetration and survival, acting thus as a contraceptive.

Thirdly, the Pill disrupts the normal growth pattern of the endometrium so that it is not capable of nurturing the embryo if fertilisation and implantation occur.

In Pills with a low dose of oestrogen (for example, 30 micrograms), the effects on sperm penetration of the mucus and on the endometrium (causing failure to implant) assume greater importance. Some studies indicate that the low-dose Pills prevent ovulation only 50 per cent of the time.

The Mini Pill, containing only a progestogen, suppresses ovulation in only 40 per cent of cycles, and relies for its contraceptive effectiveness on stimulating the production of barrier-type mucus, as well as altering the normal growth of the endometrium so that it cannot support an embryo. It may also alter the normal contractions of the Fallopian tubes and the function of the corpus luteum.

Effectiveness of the Pill

The variation in the effectiveness of the different forms of the Pill is due mainly to the amount of oestrogen present. Used as directed, the Combined Pill is virtually 100 per cent effective in preventing pregnancy,[1] and the Mini Pill about 97 per cent effective.

In practice, the failure rates are 2 to 4 per cent or more depending on the study. Inadvertent pregnancies among Pill-users are due mainly to forgetfulness, failure to correctly use back-up contraceptive methods after missing pills, incorrect use of pills (for example, starting on the wrong day or taking pills in the wrong sequence), stopping when a partner is away, running out, illness, interaction with other medications or substances, menstrual irregularities, and failure to take them due to concern about side-effects.[2]

To be effective, oral contraceptives must be taken exactly according to instruction (commonly for twenty-one out of every twenty-eight days), because the oestrogen component is broken down by the body.

Acceptability

It is important to remember that the quoted effectiveness rates apply only to the group of women who are able to tolerate the Pill. Many women cannot use oral contraceptives either because of pre-existing medical conditions or because of side-effects. Many of the adverse effects on health are related to the dosage of oestrogen—the higher the oestrogen content, the more likely are severe effects. However, progestogens may also cause problems.

It is because of these side-effects that many women discontinue the Pill. Studies have indicated that as many as 60 per cent of new Pill-users discontinue use before the end of the first year, most within the first six months.[3]

The main reason for discontinuing Pill use is the occurrence of menstrual irregularities and other side-effects. The side-effects may be either the cause or the effect of incorrectly taken Pills and may lead to discontinuation or to inadvertent pregnancy. For example, nausea in the first few months may lead to intermittent use, which in turn may provoke breakthrough bleeding, which may lead to discontinuation.[4]

When is the Pill advised against?

The International Planned Parenthood Federation (IPPF) advises women with the following conditions not to use the Pill:[5]
- clots in the legs or lungs
- previous heart attack or stroke
- known or suspected cancer of the breast, cervix, uterus or ovaries
- unusual vaginal bleeding, the cause of which has not been diagnosed
- migraine headaches
- a family history of high blood fats, including cholesterol

Furthermore, women who smoke should stop using the Pill by the age of thirty-five as the risks of heart and blood-vessel disease then become unacceptably high.

There are other situations where your doctor should carefully assess the risks and benefits before prescribing the Pill, should explain the potential risks, and should discuss possible alternative contraceptive methods. These include:

- age over forty years
- mild high blood pressure or a history of high blood pressure during pregnancy (pre-eclampsia or toxaemia of pregnancy)
- epilepsy
- diabetes
- bouts of depression in the past
- a recent tendency for menstrual bleeding to be excessive or non-existent in women who have not had any children
- gallbladder or liver disease

Pregnancy should be ruled out before starting a course of Pill tablets.

If despite these situations the Pill is used, it is particularly important for your doctor to monitor your health closely.

Adverse effects of the Pill

The Pill indisputably does what it claims to do—it prevents pregnancy. But as well as fulfilling its professed function, the Pill can do many other things—some of them very unpleasant—to your body, affecting organs other than the reproductive system. More than thirty known side-effects have been documented in medical journals, government health information bulletins, and advice from leading medical organisations such as the World Health Organisation, the Royal College of General Practitioners in

Britain, and the US Food and Drug Administration. Detailed warnings of possible side-effects are provided with Pill prescriptions in most western nations. It is advisable, even crucial, to take account of these warnings.

Since the release of the first Pill in the mid-1950s and the occurrence of unanticipated illness and death in some women, Pill manufacturers have made significant changes to its composition. Chief among these has been a substantial reduction in the amount of the widely used oestrogen called ethinyl oestradiol in Pills. Secondly, manufacturers have marketed pills with a wider choice of progestogens. As well as these changes in composition, the methods of delivering the components of the Pill have expanded. As well as pills taken by mouth, attempts have been made to deliver contraceptive hormones via intra-uterine devices (dealt with separately later in this chapter), implants, skin patches and gels.

Despite these changes, the Pill continues to pose serious health risks for women with pre-existing medical conditions, those who have major surgery that involves prolonged immobilisation, and for women who smoke. Those whose health may be endangered by Pill use include women with untreated high blood pressure, current or previous episodes of blood clots and those who experience migraines. They have an increased risk of heart attack and stroke.[6] So too do smokers, whose risk increases with age and with increasing numbers of cigarettes smoked daily. It is apparent that Pill problems still remain in spite of attempts to rectify their shortcomings.[7]

Many of the side-effects of the Pill are experienced so commonly, or are so serious, that it is worth listing some of them.

THROMBOSIS   One of the most serious problems encountered when taking the Pill is that the oestrogen component tends to increase the formation of blood clots (thrombosis).[8] Progestogen may also be involved in blood clotting, particularly in the presence of stress.[9]

The problem first became apparent in the late 1960s, after the Pill had been in general use for eight years. At that time, Oxford University researchers showed an association between use of oral contraceptives and an increased risk of blood clots affecting the veins and arteries of the legs, lungs, and brain. On the advice of the British Committee on the Safety of Drugs,[10] the oestrogen content was reduced in later formulations and is now no more than 30–50 micrograms. The progestogen level has also been reduced in third-generation pills. Nonetheless four well-designed studies have found that women taking third-generation pills have twice the risk of thrombosis of those on second-generation pills.[11,12,13,14] Published criticisms of these studies have not alleviated concerns,[15, 16, 17, 18] and an analysis that combined the results of many studies has confirmed the increased risk.[19] It is worth bearing in mind that the risk of thrombosis in women using second-generation Pills is four times that of non-Pill users, so users of the new formulations run a higher risk than ever of dangerous blood clot formation.

The formation of clots can be a serious problem when emergency surgery is required on a woman who is taking the Pill. Because of the effects on clotting, surgeons now recommend that a woman undergoing elective (non-urgent) surgery should discontinue the Pill four to eight weeks before her operation.

HEART ATTACKS   The clear identification of a relationship between heart attacks and Pill use came in the late 1960s when women were using the older, high-dose formulations.

Nevertheless there is no doubt that women who use the Pill and have one or more of the following risk factors

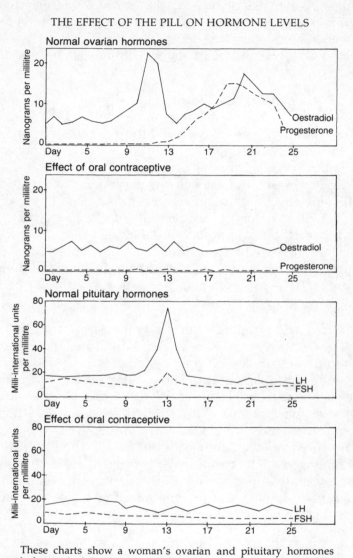

THE EFFECT OF THE PILL ON HORMONE LEVELS

These charts show a woman's ovarian and pituitary hormones before and while taking the Pill. The Pill suppresses normal levels of these hormones.

are at greater risk of heart attack:[20] aged over thirty-five years, smoking, high blood pressure, or high blood-fat levels. The relationship between current low-dose pills, blood-fat levels and heart attacks continues to be investigated.

HIGH BLOOD PRESSURE   Elevated blood pressure is sometimes seen in Pill-users and is more common the longer oral contraceptives are used and the older the woman.

Several reports suggest that the progestogen component of pills plays a part in this, and pills containing the lowest effective dose of progestogens are recommended to reduce this side-effect. Pill manufacturers recommend that users of the Pill have their blood pressure checked regularly.

Research also suggests a link between use of the Pill and an increased risk during subsequent pregnancy of high blood pressure (pre-eclampsia or toxaemia of pregnancy).[21] This is a potentially serious condition for both the pregnant woman and her baby.

STROKE   The extent to which the Pill causes stroke is no longer controversial. Recent studies indicate that women who do not smoke, do not have high blood pressure or high blood-fat levels and who use low-dose pills are not at increased risk. However, World Health Organisation studies indicate that Pill-users with uncontrolled high blood pressure are particularly susceptible to stroke compared with women who do not use the Pill.[22] In a young woman the stroke may not be fatal, but it can have a devastating impact on the patient and her family because of the lengthy rehabilitation necessary and residual physical or mental impairment.

GALLBLADDER DISEASE   Several studies have reported an increased risk of gallbladder disease in Pill-users,[23] particularly among those on the Pill for two or more years. Research suggests the Pill may accelerate the onset of gallbladder disease among some women. American and British studies indicate that the incidence of surgically proven gall stones is doubled in women on the Pill.[24]

LIVER DISEASE   The oestrogens used in the Pill cause numerous changes to the metabolism of the liver. Women with active liver disease should not take the Pill.[25]

Rarely, long-term use of the Pill is associated with a non-cancerous form of liver disease called liver adenoma. Concerns expressed in the mid-1980s that the Pill might cause liver cancer remain contentious, with considerable conflict in interpretation of the results to date.[26, 27, 28]

BIRTH DEFECTS   As long ago as the 1970s the US Food and Drug Administration advised women who suspect they are pregnant not to take oral contraceptives because of possible damage to the developing child.[29]

An increased risk of birth defects, including heart and limb defects, has been associated with the use of sex hormones, including oral contraceptives, in pregnancy.

In addition, the developing female child whose mother has received DES (diethylstilboestrol), an oestrogen formerly used to prevent early miscarriage during pregnancy, has a risk of getting cancer of the vagina or cervix in her teens or young adulthood. The risk is estimated to be about one in 1000 exposures or less.

Abnormalities of the urinary and sex organs have been reported in male offspring so exposed. It is possible that other oestrogens, such as the oestrogens in oral contraceptives, could have the same effect in the child if the mother takes them during pregnancy.

Women who wish to become pregnant may be advised to use another method of fertility control for three or four months after coming off the Pill before attempting to conceive. This is because of the increased incidence of foetal abnormalities found in miscarried babies whose mothers used the Pill immediately before becoming pregnant, although chromosomal abnormalities account for some of these. If you do become pregnant soon after stopping use of oral contraceptives—and if you do not miscarry—there is no evidence that the baby has an increased risk of abnormality. The greatest risk lies in those cases where low-dose pills are used after an unsuspected pregnancy has occurred.

BREAST MILK QUALITY AND QUANTITY   Breast milk is the best source of nutrition for infants and also protects them against some diseases. It is therefore important not to interfere with breastfeeding by inappropriate use of certain forms of contraception.

Breast-feeding mothers were advised not to use the Pill in the 1960s due to concerns that contraceptive steroid hormones could harm babies in the first few months after birth. These days, this advice is less dogmatic in the case of the Mini Pill (containing only progestogen) but concerns remain about combined pills (containing both oestrogen and progestogen). The World Health Organisation has warned that the quantity of breast milk and thus the duration of breastfeeding is reduced with the use of the combined Pill in the first six months after birth or before weaning occurs.[30] In addition, the hormones contained in the Pill have been shown to enter breast milk and thus may be absorbed by the breast-fed baby. Synthetic progesterone is known to act on the hypothalamus—an important brain centre. What effect this has on the developing infant is not yet established.

It is neither wise nor advisable to prescribe oral contraceptives to nursing mothers [our italics]. This is because the steroid components (hormones), as is the case with most drugs, are excreted into the milk. Their effects on the neonate are variable and dose-dependent. For example, an androgen-type progestogen may masculinize a female infant, and steroid metabolises may contribute to neonatal jaundice. — Dr W.N. Spellacy, Chairman, Department of Obstetrics and Gynaecology, University of Miami Medical School.

ECTOPIC PREGANCY   Use of the Mini Pill has been linked with a significantly increased risk of ectopic pregnancy (a pregnancy in a Fallopian tube, instead of the uterine cavity).[31] Use of the Combined Pill has also been linked to ectopic pregnancy, but to a lesser degree.[32] Some clinicians consider that this association has been overlooked in the medical literature and that most prescribers and dispensers of the Pill are unaware of it. They suggest that if any women on the Pill presents with pelvic pain and unusual vaginal bleeding, the presence of an ectopic pregnancy should be ruled out at an early stage.[33]

CANCER OF THE REPRODUCTIVE ORGANS   Research suggests that prolonged use, together with multiple sexual partners and hence exposure to the papilloma virus, may be associated with an increased risk of cervix cancer.[34]

A review of fourteen studies involving more than 3800 women with invasive cervical cancer found a significant increase in risk of this cancer the longer the Pill was used. The risk rose from 37 per cent above average after four years of Pill use, to 60 per cent after eight years and 77 per cent after twelve years.[35] The effect on the cervix may be due to the progression to cancer of already abnormal cells.[36] Serious cervical erosion requiring treatment is also associated with use of the Pill.

BREAST TUMOURS   Many studies indicate that women taking the Pill have a *reduced* risk of getting benign (non-cancerous) breast disease such as breast cysts. However, some studies have suggested an increased risk of breast cancer in women whose cancer was diagnosed before the age of forty-five, who have used the Pill for a long time, or who started using the Pill before the age of twenty-five and/or before their first full-term pregnancy.

In 1996 a large international collaborative group reexamined the worldwide epidemiological data on risk of breast cancer and use of the Pill. The group analysed data from fifty-four studies performed in twenty-five countries and more than 150 000 women. It concluded that women taking the Pill and those who took it within the previous five years had a 25 per cent higher than expected risk of breast cancer. The risk fell after stopping the Pill, so that ten or more years later women were no longer at significantly increased risk of breast cancer.[37] On a more positive note, the group found that the breast cancers diagnosed in women taking the Pill tended to be situated within the breast and had not spread from it. Their cancers were thus less advanced and more treatable than those in non-Pill users.[38]

MENSTRUAL IRREGULARITIES   Breakthrough bleeding between periods commonly occurs with low-dose Biphasic and Triphasic pills.[39] This may settle down within the first few months of use. The Mini Pill tends to cause continued spotting or unpredictable bleeding, or periods may stop altogether in a small number of users. Approximately 25 per cent of women prescribed the Mini Pill give it up because of unacceptable bleeding.[40]

POST-PILL INFERTILITY   This can be recognised by failure to menstruate or ovulate, or disturbance of production of the mucus with fertile characteristics. Post-pill amenorrhoea is the failure to menstruate within six months of coming off the Pill.

It appears that, following prolonged exposure to oral contraceptives, a large proportion of thick mucus is released or insufficient mucus with fertile characteristics. Since the lubricative mucus is essential for sperm fertilising capacity and transport, conception fails even though ovulation may be occurring. As yet no remedy has been found for this disturbance except time and nature.[41]

The first spontaneous ovulation after stopping the Pill is sometimes delayed, and there is evidence of temporary impairment of fertility in some women which appears to be independent of the number of years they have used the Pill.

ADOLESCENCE   Reputable clinicians have pointed out that many studies to date have not adequately addressed the effects of steroid hormones on the tissues of young women. This omission may occur if studies focus on the contraceptive behaviour of, say, women recruited in the 1960s and 1970s, rather than their counterparts in the 1980s and 1990s. The possibility of such a scenario was noted in a large Oxford analysis of many studies on breast cancer. It pointed out that only one per cent of women aged forty-five to fifty-four in 1996 took the Pill before age 20, and 54 per cent of them started on it after age 30 by which time many had children. By contrast, in women under age 35, 42 per cent first took the Pill before age 20 when many had no children, and only 2 per cent started on the Pill after turning thirty.[42] This is critical because breast and other tissues may be more vulnerable to externally introduced hormones in younger women and those who do not have children.

VITAMIN AND MINERAL STATUS   The Pill reduces blood levels of several important vitamins and minerals in some women. Research suggests there is no need for routine vitamin supplementation in Pill-users, even in populations where malnutrition is prevalent.[43] However, as the Pill may deplete iron and/or folic acid in some women, supplements may be recommended in such cases. A deficiency of folic acid is associated with neural tube defects.

INFECTIONS   The Pill appears to aggravate recurrent genital herpes and thrush.[44]

WEIGHT GAIN   Oral contraceptives alter carbohydrate metabolism in 15 to 40 per cent of women on the Pill. The hormones in the Pill tend to increase appetite, facilitate fat deposition and cause fluids to be retained which may also increase weight.[45]

MIGRAINE   If the Pill sets off migraines it should be discontinued. The headaches are sometimes related to withdrawal of oestrogen in the Pill-free week of the cycle.

NAUSEA   Many Pill-users complain of this, especially shortly after commencing the Pill. Young women who have never been pregnant, and women who tend to experience nausea during pregnancy, seem to be worst affected.

DIABETES   Changes in blood insulin levels and in glucose tolerance have also been observed in some Pill-users. Patients with a predisposition to diabetes should consider an alternative to the Pill.

DEPRESSION, IRRITABILITY, LOSS OF INTEREST IN SEX   An estimated 6 per cent of women on the Pill develop irritability, loss of libido, and depression.[46] A previous history of depression appears to predispose some women to increased symptoms. The longer the time of Pill use, the older you are, and the higher the progestogen level of the Pill, the more likely you are to suffer from these complaints.[47]

The Pill, while it protects women from the consequences of sexual relations, all too often stops them wanting any. They are afforded protection from something they no longer desire. No wonder so many women feel cheated, feel that this so-called liberator of women is just one more agent of oppression.
—Anne Summers, *Damned Whores and God's Police* (Penguin)

Changing attitudes to the Pill

When the Pill was first released amid considerable hype in Britain, the United States and Australia, no one would have guessed that its developer, Dr Carl Djerassi, would ever acknowledge the value of non-technological approaches to birth control.

But Dr Djerassi did just that in 1990,[48] aware of the

mountains of research showing the widespread nature of Pill effects on the human body. In calling for a new look at the place of natural family planning in modern society, he joined a growing chorus of voices urging a redirection of the available skills, energy and resources.

Commenting on Dr Djerassi's change of heart, the International Planned Parenthood Federation (IPPF) newsletter, *Research in Reproduction,* described the 'crisis in contraceptive research'. Large pharmaceutical companies were withdrawing from the field for reasons including claims for legal liability, stringent toxicology trials, and exceptionally long lead times between discovery of a promising product and its release onto the market.[49]

The IPPF continued:

There could well be some advantages in these proposals for improved methods of natural family planning. Many women would undoubtedly destroy their contraceptive pills with relief, the large-scale use of steroids would be averted, improvements in other forms of non-steroidal contraception such as condoms and spermicides might well enhance the effectiveness of ovulation detection, and the vast increase in knowledge of ovarian follicular physiology might lead to better markers of ovulation.

Noting Dr Djerassi's observation that most American women learn deplorably little about the menstrual cycle during their education, the IPPF mused that perhaps 'a knowledge of the time when and whether she ovulates might soon be a routine item of personal health education for each woman'.

The Intra-uterine Device (IUD), coil, loop

The IUD lost favour as liability claims in the US prompted manufacturers to withdraw various types of device from the market. The upshot is that IUDs have not become as popular as predicted, and few types are now available. Selection of women for IUD use has become a much more careful process than in the past. Women considered suitable tend to be those in a stable relationship who have completed their childbearing.

In general, IUDs work by causing an inflammatory reaction of the endometrium so that a fertilised egg cannot implant. Some types, such as those containing copper, also reduce sperm survival.

Another type of IUD contains a component of the Pill—the progestogen levonorgestrel—which is released at low levels for five years. The levonorgestrel-releasing IUD is associated with a lower risk of ectopic pregnancy than its predecessors, and also seems to reduce menstrual blood loss.[50] This is considered an important feature for women approaching the menopause who typically experience heavy periods over many months. In many cases this excessive bleeding results in inappropriate hysterectomies.

Before inserting an IUD, the doctor should take a complete medical history.[51] The doctor should conduct a physical examination, including a cervical (Pap) smear and, if indicated, should perform appropriate tests for sexually transmitted diseases. The size and position of the uterus should also be assessed.

A full check-up is essential four to six weeks after the menstrual period following IUD insertion. And, each year, a woman who has an IUD inserted should ensure she has a Pap smear as well as a medical examination to check that the IUD thread is still in place. She should know how to locate the thread and the indications for seeking medical attention, namely a missed period or unusually light period, inability to locate the thread, signs of infection such as fever, pelvic pain or tenderness, irregular vaginal bleeding or severe cramp.

EFFECTIVENESS   The method effectiveness of IUDs is estimated at between 94 and 99 per cent.[52,53] This figure does not take into account those women who are advised against using an IUD (for example, because of pelvic infection, abnormal uterine bleeding, or valvular heart disease); or those in whom it is expelled; or those who have to stop using it because of adverse effects.

SIDE-EFFECTS OF THE IUD   The incidence of pregnancy, expulsion, and removal due to side-effects, is highest in the first year of use, and drops thereafter.

An IUD may be expelled from the body either soon after it is inserted, or at a later time. The device may pass from the body without a woman being aware of the fact, leaving her with the possibility of an unexpected pregnancy.

The main disadvantages of the IUD are the risk of uterine perforation, increased bleeding and menstrual cramps, pelvic infection with the associated risk of infertility, pregnancy and the possibility of a therapeutic abortion, expulsion and ectopic pregnancy. Doctors should discuss these possibilities in detail with would-be users.

Guidelines for the use of the IUDs[54] approved by Australia's National Health and Medical Research Council stress that before inserting an IUD, doctors should alert women to the risk that IUDs may pose to future fertility through their association with pelvic inflammatory disease: insertion of the device transports disease-causing organisms from the cervix to the endometrium and beyond, where they may build up and overcome the woman's immune system.

The guidelines specify the following situations in which IUDs should never be inserted:[55,56,57]

- acute or chronic pelvic inflammatory disease
- known or suspected pregnancy
- abnormal uterine bleeding
- confirmed or suspected cancer of the genital tract
- abnormalities of the uterus since birth or fibroids that distort the uterine cavity

- a high risk of exposure to sexually transmitted diseases

Other situations that require careful thought before an IUD is inserted include:

- pelvic inflammatory disease in the past
- multiple sexual partners or a partner who has other sexual partners (this increases the risk of pelvic inflammatory disease)
- a previous ectopic pregnancy
- blood-clotting disorder
- disease of the heart valves
- heavy menstrual flow and anaemia
- severe abnormal blood loss

The guidelines stress that women who have not had any children and who are aged under twenty-five should be advised not to choose an IUD as their first method of contraception.[58]

Diaphragms, cervical caps and spermicidal chemicals

Before the Pill and the IUD became popular, the diaphragm was commonly used. When properly fitted—and this requires training by a doctor—the dome-shaped diaphragm fits over the cervix, forming a physical barrier to sperm cells. The use of spermicidal foams, jellies, or pessaries adds a chemical barrier.

The method effectiveness is estimated at 95 per cent,[59] but this figure varies widely depending on the chemical spermicide used, proper fit and care of the diaphragm and consistent and careful use. In practice, the total effectiveness is more like 80 per cent, due largely to incorrect positioning of the diaphragm or inadequate spermicidal foam.

The low continuation rate at six months[60] indicates that many couples find this method unsatisfactory. Many women complain that the diaphragm disrupts spontaneity, for unless she has planned ahead, she must insert the diaphragm immediately prior to intercourse. Some women routinely insert a diaphragm each evening to overcome this problem.

Some couples regard the messiness of the spermicidal foam or jelly that accompanies the diaphragm as a disadvantage.

Attempts to combine the diaphragm with the Billings Method have proved unsuccessful. The mucus pattern is obscured by seminal fluid and spermicidal cream, making accurate assessment of fertility or infertility difficult.

The cervical cap, a variation of the diaphragm, is shaped like small thimble and fits over the cervix. It is more rigid than the diaphragm and is held in position by suction. Manufacturers recommend that the initial fitting is performed by a medically trained person and that, before insertion, it is one-third filled with spermicidal cream. Some caps have a one-way valve that allows secretions and blood from the uterus to escape but does not permit entry of sperm.

Studies indicate that the effectiveness of the cap is about the same as that of the diaphragm, with a critical factor being the skill with which it is inserted.

The cap is unsuitable for women with erosion, malformation or infection of the cervix or for women who do not feel comfortable or confident feeling the cervix. Major disadvantages are the difficulty of insertion and removal, and the formation within the cap of a smelly secretion which indicates infection.

The condom or sheath

Used every time as directed, a high-quality condom is about 97 per cent effective.[61] Failure to use it carefully, so that some seminal fluid escapes either into the vagina, or even into the area outside the vagina, reduces the effectiveness to about 80 per cent.[62] There is a suggestion that the first pregnancy of couples who regularly use condons has an increased risk of pre-eclampsia, as the almost complete exclusion of semen from the vagina causes an aberration of the immune system.

The continuation rate at six months is about 56 per cent, and at one year only 22 per cent remain users.[63] This is an indication that many couples find the method either unsatisfactory or aesthetically unappealing. Research indicates that condoms are ineffective in excluding the eight most prevalent sexually transmitted diseases, amongst them HIV and the human papilloma virus.[64]

In addition, use of the condom may inhibit spontaneity, and may cause loss of an erection and consequent frustration. Sensation may be reduced because the penis is not directly touching the vagina.

The friction of an insufficiently lubricated condom can produce irritation in the vagina. Attempts to overcome this with lubricating chemicals may prove counterproductive: artificial agents introduced into the vagina tend to irritate the delicate lining cells, causing infection and sensitivity.

The female condom

This is a plastic pouch inserted as a lining to the whole vaginal surface. Intercourse takes place within it, aided by a lubricant. Partners report that it does not reduce the pleasurable sensations of intercourse as much as ordinary close-fitting male condoms.

A lower (vulvar) ring prevents the condom from being dislodged into the vagina, and an upper loose ring helps to ensure it stays in place.

The female condom is now available. Studies into its acceptability and effectiveness are continuing, but are not promising.[65]

The vaginal ring

This ring is designed to be inserted and removed from the vagina by users every three months. It releases a single hormone or a combination of hormones.

For example, one ring being studied releases a small dose of the progestogen levonorgestrel, and side-effects are similar to those of the Mini Pill. The most common reason for stopping use of this ring is irregular bleeding. A large multinational study found the method effectiveness to be about 96 per cent.[66] The effectiveness was lower in women weighing over 70 kg.

Contraceptive injections

Depo-Provera (medroxyprogesterone acetate), often referred to MPA or DMPA, is taken in the form of an injection every three months. It prevents pregnancy by altering the normal growth of the endometrium among other modes of action. It is thought to interfere with the hypothalamus-pituitary-ovary circuit also. The method is estimated to be 99 per cent effective. The continuation rate is about 70 per cent at one year.[67]

COMPLICATIONS Depo-Provera may cause a progressive decline in bleeding each cycle. If it continues to be used for more than two years, menstrual periods may no longer occur, probably because the endometrium is no longer capable of normal growth. Return of fertility may be delayed for months or years.[68] On the other hand, the injectible contraceptive sometimes causes heavy and unpredictable bleeding.

Other problems involve the risk of congenital malformations in children if the injection fails and a pregnancy occurs. It is also known that Depo-Provera adversely affects breast milk. Headaches, depression, loss of libido and pains in the limbs are among the adverse reactions.[69,70]

While some population agencies continue to distribute Depo-Provera widely in developing countries, various government agencies have restricted its availability. Not until 1992, several decades after its release in many other countries, did the US Food and Drug Administration give regulatory approval for marketing it.[71]

The Australian Drug Evaluation Committee states that it may be used as a contraceptive only under certain conditions. These are that the prescribing doctor must regard it as the most appropriate contraceptive method for a particular individual who has given informed consent, and the prescriber must have an adequate knowledge of the drug.

Emergency birth control

The most common approach to emergency birth control (sometimes called 'the night-after pill') is known as the Yuzpe method, which must begin within seventy-two hours of intercourse. It entails taking two lots of hormone tablets, twelve hours apart. The method effectiveness is estimated at 94 to 98 per cent.[72,73]

The method is advised against for women who are already diagnosed as pregnant, have heart problems, liver disease, undiagnosed genital tract bleeding or a history of abnormal blood clot formation. Common side-effects include nausea, vomiting and, when the method fails, ectopic pregnancy. Whereas the Yuzpe method combines oestrogen and progestogens, another method involves two doses of the progestogen known as levonorgestrel. A number of studies claim the latter approach results in fewer pregnancies and has fewer side-effects.[74,75]

RU 486   Depending on when it is taken, this drug, also called mifepristone, is used to prevent the embryo implanting, or to cause abortion of the recently implanted embryo. It has thus been described as a contragestive agent.

Termed a 'designer drug', it was the first in a new class of compounds that compete with progesterone. The initiation and maintenance of early pregnancy relies on progesterone produced by the ovaries and which acts on the uterus. By binding to the sites where progesterone usually attaches within the uterus, RU 486 interferes with early pregnancy.

When given in combination with another substance, namely a prostaglandin, RU 486 is highly effective in disrupting pregnancy within seven weeks of a missed 6eriod.[76] Bleeding lasts for from eight to fifteen days and in over 90 per cent of cases results in complete abortion. Side-effects include the need for pain relief, and occasionally blood transfusion. If the treatment fails to induce abortion or there is heavy bleeding, curettage or suction abortion follows.[77]

The 'Male Pill'

This remains elusive because of the large number of sperm that have to be neutralised, the three-month lead time until all the sperm already produced are eliminated, the possibility of damage to future sperm, and the problem of maintaining male libido at the same time as blocking conception.

While studies of regular injections of testosterone have given researchers some encouragement,[78,79,80] several practical concerns have been identified. First, the effectiveness of the testosterone-based male Pill in suppressing sperm production varies widely in different ethnic groups, and the reasons for these differences are unclear. Second, side-effects such as acne and weight gain are of concern to many men. And finally, potential long-term risks of testosterone-based male contraception have not been identified. It has been suggested that widespread acceptability and efficacy will require the development of a combination of testosterone with another steroid hormone.[81]

Skin implants

The most widely known implant, called Norplant, is a series of capsules containing a long-acting progestogen. The capsules are inserted below the skin of the arm and release their contraceptive chemical at a constant rate for about five years. Its effectiveness is estimated to be about 99 per cent.

Norplant has a triple-barrelled action suppressing ovulation in some cycles, changing the cervical mucus so that sperm cannot penetrate, and altering the endometrium so that it is no longer receptive to an embryo.

Side-effects include an increased number of days of bleeding, an unpredictable pattern of bleeding, a high risk of ectopic pregnancy, pain or rash at the site of the implant, delays in the return of fertility after discontinuing the method, excess weight gain and irrational mood changes.[82] (See also chapter 8.)

Should a woman wish to discontinue treatment, problems may arise with the removal of implants.

Sterilisation

Sterilisation is a fundamental life change and is therefore an extremely difficult and serious step.

With present surgical techniques, reversal attempts are successful only about half the time. This can prove a source of great regret should the family situation change—through death of a child or re-marriage—and another child be desired. It should be regarded as irreversible.

Female sterilisation procedures

HYSTERECTOMY   This involves removal of the uterus, and usually the cervix also. The woman continues to ovulate, but menstruation, fertilisation and implantation no longer happen.

Post-operative depression and sexual dysfunction are more common after a hysterectomy than after other operations. Fears may centre around a possible loss of femininity, loss of childbearing ability, and effects on sexuality.

The two major sexual problems following hysterectomy are loss of interest in sex, and dyspareunia (pain with intercourse). In a study of sexual response following hysterectomy and removal of ovaries, one-third of women complained of a deterioration of their sexual relationships, which they attributed to the operation.

Pelvic infection is a complication in about one per cent of cases.

TUBAL LIGATION   There are two ways of doing this, both requiring a local or general anaesthetic. In one, an abdominal incision is made, a piece of each Fallopian tube is cut out, and the two ends are tied off and folded back into the surrounding tissue. This method is often used immediately after childbirth. The second method involves entering the body through the vagina and cutting the tubes. After these procedures, menstruation continues as the uterus is still intact.

Physical complications of tubal sterilisation include severe bleeding, pelvic infection, and ectopic pregnancies. The ectopic pregnancy rate following tubal ligation is reported to be up to twenty times the normal rate. The reported incidence of menstrual problems such as heavy bleeding varies from 8 to 25 per cent. In about one-third of women who have had a tubal ligation, the blood supply to the uterus is disturbed due to interference with the blood vessels of the Fallopian tubes. This may necessitate a hysterectomy. Psychological disorders may also be a problem.

THE ENDOSCOPIC OR ELECTRO-COAGULATION TECHNIQUE   This involves burning the tubes with a small instrument introduced into the body either through an abdominal incision or through the vagina.

USE OF A CLIP OR RING TO CLOSE OFF THE FALLOPIAN TUBE   This causes the tube to become fibrous. In a small number of cases, this type of sterilisation has been reversed and a subsequent pregnancy achieved. However most doctors advise that the operation is irreversible.

Microsurgery is increasingly being used when reversal procedures are requested. However even the best surgeons are unable to reverse more than 50 per cent of these operations.

It is now the policy of some hospitals not to perform sterilisations within a few days of birth. For while domestically ideal, in that the mother is not hospitalised for an extended period, it is a time of emotional flux, during which a decision that may be regretted later might easily be made.

EFFECTIVENESS   Not surprisingly, the method effectiveness of either male or female sterilisation is up to 100 per cent in skilled hands.

Male sterilisation

The operation is called a vasectomy and involves a local anaesthetic followed by incisions in the scrotum. The doctor locates the right and left vas deferens (the tubes through which sperm from the testes travel to the penis); a piece of each is removed, and the ends tied off.

The technique of 'no scalpel vasectomy' performed

through a very small incision, has been pioneered in China and Thailand. It seems to be a quicker method with fewer complications than conventional vasectomy.[83]

Following vasectomy, the presence of sperm cells has been demonstrated for three weeks to three months, making conception possible during this time.

Techniques to rejoin the vas are being developed by microsurgeons, but even when they have been successful, normal sperm function does not always return. Doctors advise men contemplating the operation to regard it as irreversible.

COMPLICATIONS Complications of vasectomy include infection and haemorrhage. Recent research also indicates that sperm not ejaculated from the body are broken down and pass into the bloodstream. There antibodies to the retained sperm are produced. Suspected consequences include thyroid and joint disorders, heart and circulatory diseases, and diabetes.

Conclusion

Technological attempts to find new forms of contraception continue. But at each turn, the health and wellbeing of a group or groups of men and women appear to be adversely affected.

The good news is that attention is being focused increasingly on natural methods of controlling fertility. This pressure to find nature's solution has come from the community in general, as well as from scientific research teams.

The results of this reaching out towards a natural method, applicable in all circumstances of reproductive life, have proved fruitful, as the next chapter shows.

CHAPTER 14

Natural methods of fertility control

As dissatisfaction with contraceptive drugs and devices grows, increasing numbers of women are seeking a fertility control method that is natural—that does not interfere with the body's normal processes.

We now know that nature has provided various indications that ovulation is occurring, or has occurred. These indications have been studied, and several different methods of natural fertility control devised.

The main candidates are the Rhythm Method, the Basal Body Temperature Method, Multiple Indicator Methods, and the Billings Ovulation Method. How do they compare?

This chapter aims to spell out the differences between these four major categories of natural fertility control. The success of any of these methods depends primarily on how well it enables you to recognise the fertile and infertile phases of your menstrual cycle. In addition, motivation and co-operation are essential; all natural methods require that you avoid sexual intercourse (and genital contact) when you recognise fertility.

The Rhythm Method

The Rhythm Method (also known as the Calendar Method) is based on the fact that ovulation usually takes place eleven to sixteen days before the following menstrual period.

When cycles are regular, this method works well. Couples can calculate when ovulation will occur, and can avoid intercourse for some days before it, allowing for a possible five-day sperm survival time. Twenty-four hours is allowed for the life of the ovum, after which the rest of the cycle is infertile.

The calculations are based on a study of your own cycle length over six to twelve months, taking into account the shortest and longest cycles experienced.

However, as soon as any irregularity occurs—and this can happen simply as a result of emotional shock, travel, illness, after a pregnancy, or as you approach the menopause— the calculation of ovulation becomes unreliable.

Studies of the cycle length of women show that no woman is naturally regular all the time, even excluding identifiable stress situations.

The method effectiveness is 99 per cent when cycles are regular; but with irregularity it can drop to 53 per cent.[1]

The Rhythm Method is not reliable enough for most couples who wish to avoid a pregnancy. It is also unnecessarily restrictive. It has been abandoned in virtually all natural family planning programmes as a method in isolation, although it is still used combined with temperature and mucus recordings in the Sympto-Thermal Method.[2] Rhythm calculations are not part of the Billings Ovulation Method. The Basic Infertile Pattern and the Early Day Rules are applied to the woman's observations at the vulva.

The Basal Body Temperature Method (BBT)

At the time of ovulation or shortly after, there is a small but definite elevation in your body temperature. As you remember from the chapter on the menstrual cycle, this is due to an increase in the hormone, progesterone.

The basal temperature, taken daily at the same time and under the same conditions—whenever possible after a period of rest or sleep—is at its lowest level before ovulation.

After ovulation, the temperature normally rises—a significant shift being at least 0.2°C (about 0.4°F).[3]

Advocates of the Temperature Method use different approaches when estimating the infertile days for intercourse after ovulation. Some claim that a rise above a set (individually determined) temperature indicates that ovulation has occurred, while others identify this event when three temperature readings are higher than the previous six. Some advise that the temperature is taken orally, others vaginally, still others rectally.

There are several problems associated with use of the Temperature Method.

First, the temperature shift provides only a *retrospective* indication that ovulation has occurred, so you are given no warning of ovulation and of your increasing fertility. This means that to be sure of avoiding a pregnancy you need to abstain during the first part of the cycle until the temperature rise indicates that ovulation has occurred. This may involve lengthy and unnecessary periods of abstinence particularly when cycles are long or when ovulation does not take place at all—which may be the common pattern after coming off the Pill, while breast-feeding, or when approaching the menopause.

Second, the temperature readings can be misleading. Fever or excess alcohol may cause a high temperature. If you were to rely on this reading as an indication that ovulation had occurred, pregnancy could result. Some studies indicate also that even when ovulation does occur, the temperature either may not rise significantly, or may do so in steps which make accurate interpretation extremely difficult.[4]

Third, the requirement that the temperature is taken at the same time of day under resting conditions may prove difficult in many family situations; such as with a mother who gets up during the night to tend young children, or when a woman is working variable shifts, for it is important to take your temperature as soon as you wake, before any activity. The term 'basal body temperature' refers to the temperature of the body at complete rest.

The Basal Body Temperature Method is 99 per cent effective when intercourse is restricted to the interval between ovulation and menstruation, from the third day after the temperature rise.

A shift in BBT is a valuable indicator that ovulation has occurred when the cervix is not functioning normally, for example due to surgery. It usually rises too late to be of assistance when trying to conceive.

The Sympto-Thermal Method (Multiple Indicators)

The Sympto-Thermal Method combines several indicators to evaluate fertility: Rhythm calculations for early days, BBT for determining ovulation, and cervical mucus. Pain, breast tension, condition of the cervix and other physiological indicators are also used.

Many people find the Sympto-Thermal Method satisfactory during normal circumstances. Most women ovulate fairly regularly for most of their reproductive life. When a woman enters a breastfeeding phase or approaches menopause, the accent of the Sympto-Thermal Method must change and Rhythm calculations and temperature readings need to give precedence to the mucus.

In managing the early days of the cycle, if precedence is given to Rhythm observations, abstinence will increase as cycles progressively lengthen due to ovulation occurring later in the cycle. When ovulation fails to occur, abstinence will be total.

The main problem with combining methods is that if different signals of ovulation are in disagreement, confusion, anxiety and abstinence tend to result, and fertility control becomes much more complicated than it need be.

In recent years self-examination of the cervix has been added to the list of multiple indicators. The woman is taught to assess the position and firmness of the cervix and the size of the cervical opening. Changes occur under hormonal control that indicate the various phases of the cycle. Mucus is sometimes taken from the cervical canal. It is seldom used as a sole method because of its unreliability and difficulty of interpretation.

The practice raises some important objections. Women have often shown a natural reluctance towards self-examination, and the delicate lining of the cervical canal has the same structure as an internal organ and is easily damaged by a fingernail, with the possibility of infection occurring.

Touching the cervix alters the mucus production and interference with the mucus at the cervix disturbs the observations at the vulva. The mucus normally changes in its characteristics as it passes to the exterior, where the woman makes Billings Ovulation Method observations. Thus there is an incompatibility between self-examination of the cervix and the Billings Ovulation Method. (See 'Pockets of Shaw', p. 214.)

Field trials, hormonal studies and cervical biophysical studies have shown that the mucus is the most reliable signal of fertility. It is not only a sign of fertility, it *is* fertility, since without it sperm will not be able to fertilise the ovum. If a less accurate indicator is allowed to assume prime importance, it will be difficult to transfer confidence to the mucus signals when ovulation fails and the temperature ceases to rise.

LAM (Lactational Amenorrhoea Method)

The benefits of breast-feeding for control of fertility are discussed in chapter 10.

The Billings Method

As already described the basis of the method is a woman's own awareness of the mucus produced by the cervix. This provides a recognisable and scientifically validated guide to her state of fertility.

The method is applicable to all phases of reproductive life—regular cycles, irregular cycles and bleeding, breast-feeding, approaching the menopause, and after coming off the Pill. Other natural methods which rely on regularity of cycles are inadequate in many of these situations, and may fail at a time of great need.

Most women will be able to learn the method by carefully reading this book and, should any difficulties or uncertainty arise, seeking the assistance of an accredited Billings Ovulation Method teacher.

There is no doubt that an increasing number of women are finding the use of their inbuilt set of fertility signals a liberating experience.

CHAPTER 15

Scientific background of the Billings Method

The importance of the mucus as nature's signal of fertility has been recognised since the nineteenth century and used as a method for more than forty years. Scientific research has gradually unfolded its vital role in assisting new life to begin. Let us examine the fundamental findings of this research.

Phases of the cycle

The Billings Method is based on established chemical events of the menstrual cycle. The menstrual cycle can be divided into four phases:

1. *The bleeding phase or menstruation.* This is a convenient marker of the beginning and end of the cycle.

2. *The early infertile days.* These occupy a variable number of days for different women. They are prolonged for many weeks in very long cycles, and are minimal in very short cycles.

3. *The fertile phase.* During this time the cervix produces fertile mucus and the ovary releases an egg cell. This wave of fertility occupies different time spans according to the couple concerned (on average five to seven days).

4. *The late infertile days.* These begin after ovulation and the death of the egg cell. Infertility continues for the remainder of the cycle and until the cervix produces fertile mucus in the next cycle.

Hormonal events of the cycle

The changes in the mucus reflect a highly complex chain of events in the body's hormonal system.

As the cycle begins, the pituitary gland at the base of the brain starts to produce two chemical messengers, Follicle Stimulating Hormone (FSH) and Luteinising Hormone (LH).

The over-riding control of FSH and LH production occurs in the area of the brain called the hypothalamus.

The hypothalamus acts like a computer—analysing nerve signals from other areas of the brain, including those generated by emotions and environmental factors such as light and dark; as well as assessing hormone signals relevant to fertility.

The follicles (that is, the groups of immature eggs each contained in a sphere of cells) within the ovaries have a threshold requirement for FSH below which no stimulation occurs (that is, the FSH has to reach a certain level in the bloodstream before the follicles will start developing).

During the early infertile days of the cycle, the FSH level is below the threshold, and the mucus is commonly sparse and dense, or absent altogether. These days when no change occurs are recognised as a Basic Infertile Pattern of dryness or of mucus (chapter 4).

Once the FSH level passes the threshold, a group of follicles begins to develop. These follicles produce the hormone, oestrogen. At this point, if you have experienced dry days, you will notice mucus; if unchanging, opaque, sticky mucus has been evident, you will now notice that it too, reaches a point of change.

If FSH production is arrested at this intermediate stage, the follicles remain in a state of chronic minimal stimulation which may lead to the intermittent appearance of fertile-type mucus and episodes of bleeding, indicative of some growth of the lining of the uterus, the endometrium.

Ovulation is delayed until a further rise in FSH.

This situation of delayed ovulation occurs in some cycles due to stress or illness, and is common towards the end of breastfeeding, after coming off the Pill, and when approaching the menopause.

When a follicle is developing satisfactorily, it produces the hormone oestradiol, an oestrogen, which acts as a signal informing the brain of the level of ovarian activity.

In response to a high oestradiol level, the pituitary gland slows down its production of FSH and releases a series of surges of LH over a period of forty-eight hours. The dominant follicle rapidly matures and important changes take place in the chromosomes of the egg cell— which contain the inherited genetic material.

This peak LH level triggers ovulation about seventeen hours later. The LH is also responsible for the production of the corpus luteum which forms from the empty follicle and surrounding cells in the ovary after the release of the egg.

After ovulation, the corpus luteum produces the hormones progesterone and oestradiol. These are necessary for the continued growth and development of the nutritive endometrium in preparation for possible implantation should a sperm fertilise the egg.

In the absence of pregnancy, the production of these hormones declines after about six days, thus removing the hormonal support for the endometrium. When this is shed, menstrual bleeding occurs, and the cycle starts again with a rise of FSH (withdrawal bleeding).

A number of other hormones play a role in the menstrual cycle. The part played by noradrenaline, discussed later in this chapter, is assuming greater importance in the understanding of the ovulatory mechanism.

Development of the Billings Ovulation Method

In developing the method, four overlapping stages were involved:
- Careful clinical observation of women during many hundreds of cycles to establish a pattern of mucus recognisable by women and a set of guidelines for effective fertility control.
- Scientific verification of these guidelines
- Trials to establish the effectiveness of the method
- Design of a teaching programme and training of Billings Method teachers.

The first breakthrough—unscrambling the mucus changes

By the mid-1960s, the mucus was thought to be a recognisable marker of fertility in about 80 per cent of women only. As a result, Rhythm calculations and temperature measurements were also taught where mucus awareness alone did not appear adequate.

However, two problems remained.

Using Rhythm calculations, seven days at most at the beginning of the cycle could be considered infertile, and thus available for intercourse. This imposed severe restrictions during breastfeeding, naturally occurring long cycles, and in the years approaching the menopause when cycles tend to be long and ovulation is an increasingly rare event. (Some attempts were made to shorten cycles artificially using hormones—an approach we rejected. We also resisted the practice of advising young mothers to stop feeding their babies so that they would ovulate.)

Couples who relied on a temperature rise to indicate

post-ovulatory infertility often faced long periods of unnecessary abstinence when ovulation was greatly delayed or did not occur at all.

The solutions to both these problems were found by paying greater attention to the mucus observations and sensations of women themselves.

It became apparent that when women taught each other the Billings Method, virtually all women (not 80 per cent, as the male teachers had thought) were able to produce a recognisable mucus pattern. This meant that mucus observations alone were adequate for the detection of ovulation.

It was also noticed that before the mucus began its rapid development leading to the Peak, many women were experiencing a 'positive sensation of nothingness', which they referred to as 'dry days'.

The concentrated investigation of all the 'difficult cases'—that is, breastfeeding mothers and premenopausal women—led to a detailed study of the long anovulatory situations. It was gradually appreciated that dryness or an unvarying scant discharge continued for a long time until a few days before ovulation, and was then replaced by mucus with fertile characteristics. The number of dry days or days of unchanging mucus was seen to vary according to the length of the cycle—being greater in cycles when ovulation was delayed.

It was at last appreciated that the mucus observations and sensations could tell a woman all she needed to know of fertility both before and after ovulation. The problem of the long cycle, that is, the cycle in which ovulation was delayed, was thus solved.

The refinement of the Billings Method led to the progressive elimination of temperature-taking, which many women themselves initiated, during the late 1960s. All attention was given to the signs of the mucus. Following this, a rapid increase in knowledge of the mucus as an indicator of fertility or gynaecological abnormalities occurred. For the first time the 'problem cases' were solved, and it remained only to verify and disseminate this information by organising a competent teaching service.

Hormone studies

Much of the early key research into the method was carried out by Professor James Brown from Melbourne University and Professor Henry Burger from Monash University.

In 1962, Professor Brown commenced hormonal studies in Melbourne with the aim of assessing the validity of the mucus observations and sensations as indicators of fertility.[1] Professor Brown had earned the name Mr Oestrogens while assistant director of the Clinical Endocrinology Research Unit at Edinburgh University, where his work involved helping sub-fertile couples achieve a pregnancy. This was found to be possible by timing intercourse to coincide with laboratory measures of the peak level of the hormone oestrogen.

Working in conjunction with other researchers engaged in the visualisation of the abdominal and pelvic organs by laparoscopy, Professor Brown also helped establish the relationship between oestrogen and progesterone hormones, the cervical mucus changes, and ovulation. He concluded that the use of the mucus as a signal of fertility or infertility, and the guidelines of the Billings Ovulation Method, had a sound scientific basis. (See p. 215.)

During the same period Professor Burger, Director of Prince Henry's Institute of Medical Research in Melbourne, was engaged in pioneering work on other hormones which regulate the menstrual cycle. These include Follicle Stimulating Hormone (FSH) and Luteinising Hormone (LH).

The first report of the work relating hormone changes to the mucus symptom was published in *Lancet*, the British medical journal.[2] This report established the relationship between the surge of LH, ovulation, and the observation of the Peak mucus signal by a group of women. These findings were later confirmed by Flynn[3] in Britain, Casey[4] in Australia, Cortesi[5] in Italy, Hilgers[6] in the United States, and since 1980, by many others.

Further studies of these relationships have been conducted under the direction of the World Health Organisation's expanded program of research, development, and research training in human reproduction.

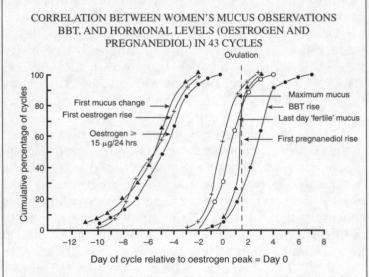

CORRELATION BETWEEN WOMEN'S MUCUS OBSERVATIONS BBT, AND HORMONAL LEVELS (OESTROGEN AND PREGNANEDIOL) IN 43 CYCLES

Cumulative percentage of cycles in which the events shown had occurred by a particular day. Days are numbered from the day of the pre-ovulatory oestrogen peak = day 0. The vertical dotted line indicates the best estimate of the moment of ovulation, which has a degree of uncertainty of approximately ± 12 hours. (*Brown, Harrison, Smith* and *Burger*)

The available evidence indicates that:

- The oestradiol spurt resulting in fertile-type mucus that warns of possible fertility, starts on average six days before ovulation.
- The oestradiol peak occurs about thirty-seven hours before ovulation.
- The LH level begins to rise about thirty to forty hours before ovulation, reaching a peak about seventeen hours before the egg cell is released. This has proved not as reliable as ovarian hormonal assays and the Peak mucus symptom.
- The Peak mucus signal, as judged by women themselves, occurs on average 0.6 day (fourteen hours) before ovulation. Occasionally ovulation may be delayed until the second day past the Peak. The diagram opposite illustrates these relationships.

As noted elsewhere, Professor Brown has made approximately 800 000 ovarian hormonal measurements in various research projects.[7]

Mucus studies

Studies of the cervical mucus, particularly in relation to infertility research, have confirmed that the mucus must have special characteristics if sperm are to reach and fertilise an egg.[8] These special characteristics give the fertile mucus its lubricativeness, and its stringy, raw egg-white appearance.

Since the late 1950s, Professor Erik Odeblad and his colleagues at the University of Umea in Sweden have investigated the biological and physical properties of the cervical mucus.[9] They demonstrated that three different types of mucus are produced by specialised parts of the cervix during the menstrual cycle. This mucus production is under the control of hormones, in particular, oestrogen

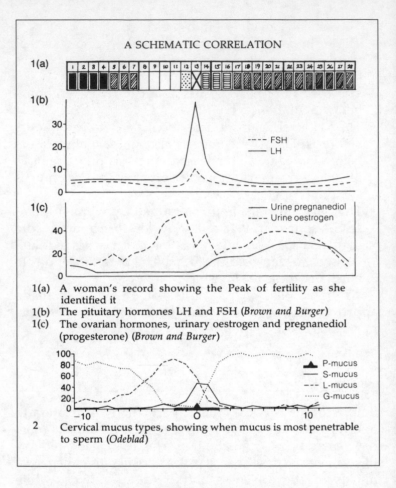

A SCHEMATIC CORRELATION

1(a) A woman's record showing the Peak of fertility as she identified it

1(b) The pituitary hormones LH and FSH (*Brown and Burger*)

1(c) The ovarian hormones, urinary oestrogen and pregnanediol (progesterone) (*Brown and Burger*)

2 Cervical mucus types, showing when mucus is most penetrable to sperm (*Odeblad*)

and progesterone. Recently a fourth type of mucus has been identified—the P-mucus.

The different types of mucus either impede or encourage the movement of sperm through the reproductive system. The relative amount of each type is crucial in determining a woman's state of fertility.

The rising oestrogens stimulate the cervix to produce the fluid L-mucus. This causes a change in sensation at

MUCUS PRODUCTION IN THE CERVIX

S-type mucus

L-type mucus

S-mucus
L-mucus
S-mucus
L-mucus
S-mucus
L-mucus

G-type mucus

Stringy S-type mucus on a glass slide showing loafs of L-type mucus

These illustrations show the distinctive structure of the three types of mucus produced by the cervix.

The S-type mucus forms channels for easy sperm transport. The L-type mucus allows partial penetrability and collection of defective sperm cells. The G-type mucus forms an impenetrable barrier.

At ovulation, S mucus predominates. After ovulation, the proportion of impenetrable G mucus increases rapidly. *(after Odeblad)*

the vulva—a change from the Basic Infertile Pattern. This mucus will be mixed with G-mucus that has been dislodged from the cervix by the wet L-mucus. *The sensation will be wet or sticky*; P-mucus is involved.

Closer to ovulation, when the L-mucus is mixed with S-mucus, strings of mucus may be pulled out. The L-mucus can be seen as beads in the clear S-mucus. The *vulval sensation is now wet and slippery.*

Closer still to ovulation, the mucus loses most or all of its stretch due to the addition of the potassium-rich P-mucus, together with the enzyme from the lower uterus

S-mucus showing channels for the progress of sperm cells; L-mucus for capturing defective or low-quality cells *(after Odeblad)*

(isthmus), which dissolves the mucus strings. The sensation is now *intensely lubricative and wet.*

It is not necessary for the woman to identify the various types of mucus visually. It is important for her to observe and record the *changing sensations* at the vulva.

Stretchiness does not identify the Peak. The last very slippery feeling identifies the Peak.[10]

When a sample of mucus is taken from the cervix close to the Peak, spread out gently on a glass slide and allowed to dry at room temperature and then viewed under the microscope, it will show the L-mucus crystallised in a delicate fern-like pattern. The remarkable function of the L-mucus is that besides providing a support for the S-mucus, it catches and eliminates defective and poor-quality sperm cells, thereby providing a perfect sperm cell for fertilisation of the ovum. Crystallisation of the S-mucus appears as fine parallel

MUCUS PRODUCTION IN THE CERVIX

L-mucus capturing
defective sperm

The interior of the cervix showing the formation of four types of
mucus in separate crypts. The fertile mucus (S), produced in the
upper crypts, forms watery channels for the transport of sperm.
The P-mucus occurs closest to the Peak. It is intensely lubricative
and does not stretch. The L-mucus eliminates defective sperm and
provides a scaffolding to support the S-mucus. The impenetrable
G-mucus is formed in the lowest crypts. It occupies the canal
during most of the cycle, preventing sperm entry. (*After Odeblad*)

needles indicating the channels that provide rapid
sperm transport.

Usually on the day of the Peak symptom, but sometimes a short time after, in the uppermost 'dome-like' area
of the cervical canal, a small quantity of P-mucus, which
is distinctly different from S- or L-mucus, is produced. It
crystallises in small hexagonal forms, because of its high
potassium content. It is responsible for an extremely
slippery sensation at the vulva. At this point the mucus
has practically no strings due to the addition of the
P-mucus acting with the zymogen (enzyme) granules

from the lower uterus. There is at this time, just after the oestrogen peak, a surge of noradrenaline. This hormone explains the high-activity behaviour women experience sometimes at ovulation. Heart rates have also been shown to be influenced by noradrenaline.

It is the P-mucus that gives the sperm cells their final impetus towards the uterine cavity, from whence they proceed eventually to the Fallopian tubes.

Professor Odeblad showed that the channels in the S-mucus promote the passage of sperm prior to the Peak, and for two or three days after. He has also shown that sperm may proceed directly to the uterus and Fallopian tubes, or may remain for a time in the specialised folds within the cervix where the S-type mucus is produced and where they have been locked in for a few days by the L-mucus until liberated by the P-mucus and enzyme. These 'resting' sperm cells appear to be given the final impetus to reach the uterus. *This mechanism of rest and reactivation explains how the life of sperm may be prolonged for several days after a single act of intercourse.* Once the sperm cells reach the uterus and Fallopian tubes they do not live for long.

Professor Odeblad found that the fertile S-type mucus usually *begins* to be locked into the cervical canal by the G-type mucus just prior to ovulation. However, some channels persist for a day or two after ovulation, making possible the fertilisation of an egg cell.[11]

Professor Odeblad has demonstrated that the Pockets of Shaw in the lower end of the vagina produce manganese under the influence of progesterone, which is rising just prior to ovulation. This manganese thickens any S-mucus which may still be leaving the cervix. The observations at the vulva are therefore different from observations made at the cervix. *The woman should not investigate the cervix or vagina.*

The prediction of ovulation from a woman's own

mucus observations can be confirmed by an ultrasound picture. Ultrasound is the technique for obtaining an image of various body organs by sound waves. During the week before ovulation the follicle containing the egg grows to a diameter of 24 mm. The diagram below illustrates an actual example. An ultrasound picture taken daily provided these measurements, which correlate closely with the woman's mucus record.[12]

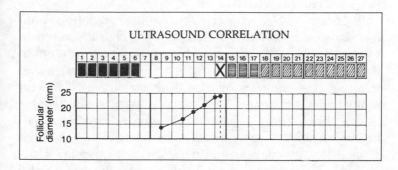

Professor J. B. Brown's Ovarian Meter

Over the years many devices have been developed around the world that measure hormones, substances in cervical mucus and its viscosity. Saliva testing has been investigated. Changes in vaginal blood flow and the body's electrical charges have been studied, all with a view to finding a simple, accurate indicator of fertility. Already many have passed into history, due to diverse difficulties including high cost and unreliability. A test that measures the peak levels of the Luteinising Hormone (LH) and indicates the imminence of ovulation has been found to be useful in cases of infertility, but it does not predict ovulation soon enough to give the necessary indications to avoid conception.

For the vast majority of women, their own observations of the mucus are simple, readily available, and a reliable guide to their fertility; no devices of any kind are necessary.

There are, however, temporary problems confronting some women that can be solved quickly by the help of accurate measurements of the ovarian hormones: for example, infertility, when the problem is a very sparse mucus secretion, can be helped through pinpointing ovulation precisely by hormonal studies. Sometimes a very anxious woman may benefit from the reassurance of the hormonal verification. Occasionally diseases of the cervix may render observations difficult for a time.

In order to help women who are in any doubt about the significance of their mucus, Professor J. B. Brown of Melbourne University developed a kit that women themselves can use. It has proved to be a valuable aid to teachers of the Billings Method and to women,[13,14] and for many it needs to be used only once or twice in a cycle. This device, the Ovarian Meter, measures the ovarian hormones oestrogen and progesterone in urine. It is easy for the woman to use at home and eliminates hospital visits and blood tests. It has been trialled by the World Health Organisation and other centres, and found to determine ovulation more accurately than fertility kits that depend on measurements of the Luteinising Hormone. The meters are available from Billings Method teaching centres.

The latest version of the meter (Mark VI) is more fully automatic: it prompts the woman to proceed with the various steps involved, and does the required calculations for her. The hormone levels can be interpreted to define the following:
- Pre-ovulatory infertile levels of oestrogen.
- The beginning of the fertile phase marked by a rise in oestrogen.
- Ovulation identified by the Peak of the oestrogens and a sudden drop.
- The beginning of the post-ovulatory infertile days identified by a rise in progesterone.

When the woman's cervix is responsive to ovarian

hormones the mucus observations correspond, and follow the hormonal patterns.

The response of the reproductive organs to the hormones is necessary for fertility. The hormones are responsible for stimulating the various reproductive organs to fulfil their functions—ovarian follicles, Fallopian tubes, endometrium, cervix, vagina.

Ovary   The FSH from the pituitary gland causes follicles in the ovary to grow and produce oestrogen until the pituitary hormone LH causes ovulation and the formation of the corpus luteum.

Endometrium   Oestrogen primes the endometrial growth which is completed by progesterone and oestrogen after ovulation for the reception of the embryo following fertilisation. When there is no fertilisation, the levels of oestrogen and progesterone fall with the shedding of the endometrium as a 'withdrawal bleed'. Preovulatory bleeding may occur due to a high level of oestrogen; this may be a 'breakthrough' bleed when the level is high and a 'withdrawal bleed' when a high level of oestrogen falls. A woman who is breastfeeding or approaching the menopause may experience several such episodes before ovulation.

Cervix   The secretion of G mucus is stimulated by progesterone. The oestrogen governs the role of the cervix in producing mucus, which is necessary for sperm selection and propagation.

As a woman approaches menopause, a raised oestrogen level may fail to produce a mucus response due to ageing of the cervix. In this case she may ovulate but remain infertile because there is no mucus to sustain the sperm.

Vagina   When there is a low oestrogen level, the usually multi-layered vaginal wall is thinned and, in the absence of cervical activity, the vulva is dry. When the oestrogen level rises, but only to a moderately low level, there is a growth of vaginal cells which are shed and broken down to produce the Basic Infertile Pattern (BIP) of an unchanging discharge. This discharge may be continuous or be interrupted by dry days as the oestrogen level fluctuates—the combined BIP.

CHAPTER 16

Trials of the method

This chapter outlines the trials of the Billings Method which were carried out in a number of countries from the 1970s onwards. More detail will be found in the references cited.

First, an explanation of some of the terms used frequently in trials.

Trials terminology

THE METHOD-RELATED PREGNANCY RATE   This indicates the number of pregnancies, expressed as a percentage, occurring when couples carry out correct instructions for a particular method. The correctly assessed pregnancy rate under these circumstances is an indication that the method has not covered a percentage of biological circumstances.

All fertility control methods have such failures, including the Pill, the IUD, and even sterilisation (chapter 13). The reasons for these failures are generally unknown.

Trials indicated that the method-related pregnancy rate for the Billings Method up until 1980 was between 0 and 2.9 per cent. This means that of 100 women using the method for a year *who consistently followed the guidelines* between none and three became pregnant.

THE TEACHING-RELATED PREGNANCY RATE   This figure applies to pregnancies resulting from incorrect teaching of a method, or to misunderstanding by the user of the method.

The user carries out the instructions as she or he understands them, but the misunderstanding is apparent to an experienced teacher or doctor.

With regard to the Billings Method, this figure in the trials varied between 0 and 6 per cent. Such variations depend largely on the calibre of the teaching, which has been continually refined and updated. Where the teacher is committed to the success of the method and is competent and experienced, the teaching-related failure rate has been reduced to near zero.

CONTINUATION RATE   This is a guide to the acceptability of a method and is judged by the readiness of users to continue with a method over an extended period and to return to a particular method after a pregnancy. The willingness to continue with the method after a pregnancy indicates that the circumstances of the pregnancy were understood and were under the control of the couple.

Because their fertility is intact, both the options to avoid or achieve a pregnancy are open to users, and they may decide to change their options from time to time.

Generally, where teaching is good, the trials of the Billings Method show a high continuation rate.

THE TOTAL PREGNANCY RATE   This total figure included pregnancies resulting from a failure of a particular method to cover all biological circumstances, misunderstanding of the method, risk-taking by couples, ambivalence towards pregnancy, and the decision by a couple to exercise the second option of achieving a pregnancy.

Within the total pregnancy rate there may also be a

number of pregnancies resulting from an act of intercourse when agreement fails between partners.

In any trial of any fertility control method a participating couple may choose to ignore the guidelines.

Personal or family reasons may lead a couple to opt out of a trial by ignoring the instructions for effective use of the particular method under study. This is the right of all couples: without this guiding principle, individual needs are displaced.

The total pregnancy rate in trials of the Billings Method varies between about 1 per cent and 25 per cent. This is to say that about between 1 and 25 pregnancies occur among one hundred couples participating in a Billings Method trial for a year.

The Billings Method allows the option to avoid as well as to achieve a pregnancy and thus the total pregnancy rate is relatively high, and varies considerably from trial to trial. Some other fertility control methods, for example sterilisation, injectables and implants have a lower total pregnancy rate because they do not allow couples the second option to the same degree.

THE PEARL INDEX   Most of the pregnancy rates quoted for the Pill, IUD, condom, and other fertility control methods are Pearl Index figures. These refer to the various types of pregnancy rate and indicate the number of pregnancies occurring for each '100 women-years' of use (that is, 100 women for one year, 50 women for two years, ten women for ten years).

One problem with this figure is that the longer the follow-up of participating women, the better the Pearl Index figure looks. This is because those who are going to become pregnant tend to do so early on—either because they take chances, misunderstand the method, are ambivalent about having children, or because the particular method under study fails to cover their biological circumstances.

The longer one follows up the women the lower the rate gets. Furthermore in initiating studies to measure effectiveness, if those who have been practising the method for several years are allowed to enrol, the apparent effectiveness will be much greater than if the study were limited to the new contraceptors. This is true even if you adjust for age, parity, and all the other demographic variables which we know will influence the Pearl Index.[1]

Robert Potter of Brown University, USA, comments: 'By allowing the successful contraceptors to contribute long-enough histories, a respectable Pearl Index pregnancy rate can be wrested from almost any sample.'[2]

To overcome weakness of the Pearl Index, other assessment methods have been devised, mainly aimed at taking account of the discontinuation rate as well as the pregnancy rate. Such methods are termed 'life table analyses' and are used more frequently in current reports.

The discontinuation rate gives some indication of whether side-effects are common, and whether couples find the method satisfactory to use.

Thorough assessment

In assessing the value of any fertility control method, it is important to examine carefully trial figures, teaching materials and attitudes, the motivation of couples, acceptability, and any physical and psychological side-effects.

Thus, for example, trial results of the Pill do not usually include a total failure rate (the oft-quoted one per cent failure rate of the Pill refers to the biological method failure rate). In studies which include those women who were unable or unwilling to tolerate the Pill and abandoned it as a means of contraception, the total pregnancy rate is as high as 20 per cent in a year.[3]

Published trials

The first published trials of the Billings Method took place on Tonga in the Pacific in 1970–72[4] and the last in China in the late 1990s.[5] In the intervening years, trialling was undertaken in Australia,[6,7] Korea,[8] India,[9,10] Ireland,[11] the USA,[12,13] Africa,[14] and Indonesia.[15] In the mid-1970s, the World Health Organisation (WHO) also conducted a five-nation trial in India, the Philippines, El Salvador, New Zealand and Ireland, to test the method among diverse socio-economic and cultural groups.[16]

From the earliest trials, as noted elsewhere, method-related pregnancy rates were as low as 0–4 per cent. As teaching methods were refined and updated, these rates fell close to zero. Continuation rates were consistently high.

It is generally accepted that the acquisition of BOM knowledge by the participants, the women's motivation and the husbands' co-operation are the key points for the successful implementation of the Billings Method.[17]

The focus of the trials varied. An early Melbourne study, for example, involved ninety-eight women between ages 38 and 54 who were judged to be approaching the menopause and who wished to find a natural solution to their family-planning problems. The method-related pregnancy rate was zero, confirming that the pattern of the cervical mucus provides women approaching the menopause with a reliable means of assessing their current state of fertility or infertility. As for acceptability— one woman required a hysterectomy when abnormalities were detected; no others discontinued.

A twelve-month multicentre study in China which included couples of different social status in rural and urban Nanjing, considered the effectiveness of the Billings Method in avoiding pregnancy when compared with the IUD and the combined use of the Billings Method and the IUD. The method-related pregnancy rate of the Billings Method group was zero, and their continuation rate was significantly higher than those in the IUD group (89.3 per cent for the IUD and 96.4 per cent for the Billings Method).

According to one continuing study of the use of the

Billings Method in cases of infertility that has no apparent cause, 1032 out of 3268 women became pregnant after two to five cycles, although many had been apparently infertile for more than five years. Amongst the remaining couples, more pregnancies can be expected eventually.

Conclusion

The trials continued to show low levels of pregnancies attributable to faults in the Billings Method. It was demonstrated that the method is applicable to all phases of reproductive life, beneficial in the solution of seeming infertility and useful in diagnosing reproductive abnormalities.

The most common cause of pregnancy is the couple's decision to have a baby, which knowledge of the fertile signs readily enables them to do—hence the variability of the total pregnancy rate exhibited in the trials.

The benefits of the method go far beyond accuracy in regulating fertility. The need to become aware of the signs of natural fertility and infertility adds another dimension to the relationship between couples as they agree to wait sometimes in order to achieve their aims for fertility control. The bond between them strengthens and the family becomes stable and secure. Rather than something that 'just happens' between them, the physical sexual relationship becomes part of a powerful communication.

Self test

It is a basic principle of the Billings Method that your own natural and easily recognisable signs are all you need to study in order to meet your reproductive needs. The following checklist of questions and answers is intended to help you focus on the most important points and may help you to better understand and apply the method.

1 How can the Billings Method be used to achieve a pregnancy?
2 How can the method be used to avoid a pregnancy?
3 Can the Billings Method be used when you are not ovulating?
4 Do all charts of the mucus look the same?
5 Will your own consecutive charts be similar?
6 What is meant by charting your normal cycle?
7 Is internal examination a useful method of mucus observation?
8 Describe the two major types of sensation you experience in a cycle.
9 Describe the mucus with fertile signs.
10 Why should sexual intercourse be avoided during the first month of charting?
11 When do you make your mucus observations?
12 When do you record your observations?
13 What do you record on your chart?
14 How long does it take to establish a Basic Infertile Pattern in an unfamiliar situation such as when approaching the menopause?

15   What is the Peak mucus?
16   How is the Peak identified?
17   For how long after the Peak should intercourse be avoided?
18   How could genital contact without sexual intercourse during days of mucus with fertile characteristics result in a pregnancy?
19   What is the Basic Infertile Pattern?
20   Are the days of menstruation available for sexual intercourse?
21   What time of day is available for intercourse during the Basic Infertile Pattern?
22   What may be the effect of stress on a woman's menstrual cycle?

Answers

1   By identifying the fertile days of the menstrual cycle, especially near the day of Peak mucus, and using these for sexual intercourse.

2   By identifying fertile days of the menstrual cycle and avoiding sexual intercourse and genital contact at these times.

3   Yes; the method is applicable to all circumstances of reproductive life. In the absence of ovulation, the method would indicate bleeding and an almost uninterrupted infertile phase.

4   No; because each woman's mucus pattern is individual to her, charts vary considerably.

5   Similar patterns *may* appear consecutively, although this is not necessarily the case.

6   Mucus observations are made by awareness of sensations during normal activities, and noticing visual characteristics of the mucus at the vaginal opening.

7   No; internal examination may cause confusion because the inside of the vagina is always moist. It may also cause infection or be culturally unacceptable. In addition, the lining of the cervix can easily be damaged.

8   Either a dry or a sticky sensation; or a wet, damp or slippery, lubricative sensation.

9   It may be wet, clear, stretchy, stringy and possibly blood-stained. It has a lubricative sensation and has the consistency and appearance of raw egg-white. You may have very little mucus. You may not see it but will feel the lubrication.

10   This is necessary in order to obtain a clear picture of the mucus, since seminal fluid or vaginal secretions may be lost from the vagina even the day after intercourse. This could conceal the presence of mucus with fertile characteristics.

11   Throughout the day, in the course of normal activities.

12   At the *end* of the day.

13   All the relevant observations of the day *plus* the appropriate symbol, *plus* a description of the most fertile characteristics of the mucus, NB sensation.

14   Two weeks observation is necessary in a long cycle.

15   This occurs on the last day of the slippery mucus and occurs when fertility is maximal.

16   It is identified retrospectively, on the following day when the sensation is no longer slippery, and dry or sticky days occur.

17   Three days.

18   A drop of semen may escape from the penis, and the fluid may contain sperm cells which could fertilise an egg.

19   Either dry days, or days of unchanging discharge, after menstruation and before ovulation.

20   No; because in a short cycle ovulation may occur before or immediately after bleeding is finished. Thus the fertile mucus may be concealed by the bleeding.

21   Intercourse should be confined to the evenings if the aim is to avoid pregnancy; this enables you to confirm that the Basic Infertile Pattern has been recognised on that day.

22   Ovulation, and its mucus indications, may be delayed.

Teaching centres

ARGENTINA

Centro Billings Merlo
Saavedra 749 (1722)
Merlo
Buenos Aires

AUSTRALIA

Head Office:

Billings Family Life Centre
27 Alexandra Parade
North Fitzroy Vic. 3068
Tel. 03 9481 1722
Fax. 03 9842 4208
Toll free 1800 335 860 (outside
  Melbourne metropolitan area)
Email: billings@ozemail.com.au

There are accredited teachers in
every state who can be contacted
as follows:

Victoria

Ballarat	03 5335 6229
Beechworth	03 5727 0224
Geelong	03 5243 9779
Mildura	03 5024 5205

N.S.W.

Sydney	02 9399 3033
Albury	02 6025 4846
Casino	02 6663 1308
Dubbo	02 6882 3084
Gosford	02 4341 5509
Newcastle	02 4979 1196
Wagga	02 6922 3215
Young	02 6382 2750

A.C.T.

Canberra	02 6239 7655
Farrer	02 6286 1720

Qld

Brisbane	07 5444 8085
Cairns	07 4054 1392
Toowoomba	07 4635 7960
Townsville	07 4772 7799

S.A.

Adelaide	08 8369 2232
Tumby Bay	08 8688 1889

W.A.

Perth	08 9337 8737
Bunbury	08 9791 3696

Tas.

Hobart	03 6221 7001
Launceston	03 6339 2230

N.T.

Darwin	08 8948 2722
Katherine	08 8972 3610

BANGLADESH
Natural Family Planning Centre
43 Testuri Bazar, Tejaon
Dhaka–1215

CANADA
Billings Method Centre
1506 Dansey Avenue
Coquitlam B.C. V3K 3J1

Natural Family Planning
3050 Young Street #205
Toronto, Ontario

Billings Method Centre
1262 Hillcrest Avenue
London, Ontario N5Y 4N4

Natural Family Planning Centre
Suite 206
1916 Second Street SW,
Calgary, Alberta T25 153

CHILE
Professor Dr Pilar Vigil
Catholic University of Chile
P.O. Box M-D
Santiago
Fax: 562 206 7929

CHINA
Anhui BOM Teaching Centre
92 Tuan Jie Road
Wuhu 241001

Beijing BOM Teaching Centre
1-1-601 Xingdao Jiayuan
Beijing 100176

Chengdu BOM Teaching Centre
24 Dongchenggen Xia Street
Chengdu 610031

Guangdong BOM Teaching
  Centre
17 Meidong Road
Guangzhou 510600

Hong Kong BOM Teachin
  Centre
Unit 112, Lee Tsui House
Wan Tsui Estate
Chai Wan
Hong Kong

Jilin BOM Teaching Centre
2 Yuandong Road
Chanchun 130041

Jinan BOM Teaching Centre
9 Shunyu Road
Jinan 250002

Macau BOM Teaching Centre
A 8F Nanbang Building
763 Nanwan Parade
Macau

Nanjing BOM Teaching Centre
  of Excellence
73–2 Jiefang Road
Nanjing 210016

Qingdao BOM Teaching Centre
90 Xuzhou Road
Qingdao 266071

Shaanxi BOM Teaching Centre
12 Taiyang Miaomen Street
Xi'an 710002

Shanghai BOM Teaching Centre
2140 Xietu Road
Shanghai 200032

Shanxi BOM Teaching Centre
12 Beiyuan Street
Taiyuan 030006

Yunnan BOM Teaching Centre
5 Jinfeng Garden
Kunming 650021

COLUMBIA
CENPAFAL
Avenida 28, no. 37–21
Apartado
Aereo no. 54569
Bogota, D.E. Columbia

CROATIA
Mariji Zivkovic
Hercegovacka 45
Hrvatska 4100
Zagreb, Croatia

DENMARK
Billings Method Centre
Rodovrevej 167/2
2610 Rodovre

EGYPT
Committee of Natural Family
  Planning
Box 73, Faggalah,
Cairo 11523

ENGLAND
The BOM Trust Natural Family
  Planning
Billings Family Life Centre
58B Vauxhall Grove
London SW8 1TB

National Association of Ovulation
  Method Instructors (NAOMI)
  UK
Dr Helen Davies, President
4 Southgate Drive, Crawley
West Sussex RH10 6RP

ETHIOPIA
Ethiopian Catholic Family Life
P.O. Box 2454
Addis Ababa

FIJI
Responsible Parenthood Council
Box 5175
Raiwaqa

FRANCE
Centre Billings France
Allée de Bois Perineau
78120 Rambouillet

GERMANY
Naturliche Familienplanung
Albert-Schweitzer-Weg 1
5220 Waldbrol

HOLLAND
Natural Family Planning
Vrenkeweg 2
6367 H J Voerendahl

INDIA
SERFAC
140 Manimangalam Road
Varadarajapuram
Chennai 600 048

Handmaids of the Blessed Trinity
Rd Z # 2 Saliar Village
Mumbai 99

INDONESIA
Yaasan Reksa Keluarga
Kotak Pos 81
Yogyakarta D.I.Y. 55001

IRELAND
N.A.O.M.I/D.O.M.A.S
16 North Great George's Street
Dublin 1

ITALY
Centro Studi e Ricerche sulla
   Regolazione Naturale della
   Fertilita
Universita Cattolica del S. Cuore
Largo Agostino Gemelli 8
00168 Roma

JAPAN
Catholic Family Centre
Sarayama 4–14–27
Minami-ki
Fukuoka City 815

KENYA
Nazareth Hospital
P.O. Box 49682
Nairobi

KIRABATI
Christian Family Life Centre
P.O. Box 20
Teaoraereke, Tarawa

KOREA
Ovulation Method Centre
225–1 Namsan 3 dong
Chung-gu 700–443
Taegu

LEBANON
Billings NFP Centre
BP 1667 Jounieh
Lebanon

LITHUANIA
Dr J. Tartiliene
Z Lianksmino 5
2001 Vilnius

MALAYSIA
Chan Lek-Lim
Box 1641
Kuching
Sarawak

MEXICO
Centro Nacional Billings de
   Mexico
Calle Luis Babrera # 844
Colonia Miraflores C.P. 44270
Guadalajara, JAL

NIGERIA
Pro-Life Family Association
P.L.A.N. National Headquarters
P.O. Box 3086
Ibadan
Oyo State

PAKISTAN
Catholic Catechetical Centre
P.O. Box 7172
Karachi–74400

PAPUA NEW GUINEA
St Paul's Pastoral Centre
P.O. Box 113
Alotau
Milne Bay Province

PARAGUAY
Casilla de Correo 227
Asuncion

PERU
Octavio Espinoza 475
San Isidro 27
Lima

PHILIPPINES
BOMPHIL
Box 191EA
Ermita
Manila 1040

POLAND
Magdalene & Andrey Winkler
44–203 Rybnik, ul PO
Walen 7

SCOTLAND
Scottish Assoc. of NFP
C/o Archdiocesan Offices
196 Clyde Street
Glasgow G1 4JY

SINGAPORE
Singapore N.F.R Service
C/o 260 Lorong Chuan
Singapore 1955

SLOVAKIA
Stefan Horvath
Hrubonova 31/21
Cs-034–1 Ruzomberok
Slovaki

SOUTH AFRICA
FERMASA
P.O. Box 941
Pretoria 0001

SPAIN
Organizacion Mundial del
  Metodo de la Ovulacion Billings
C/o Jose Calvo
23 Bajo C
28039 Madrid

SUDAN
Ms Nyanawut Mayen Kuol Deng
St Mathew Cathedral
P.O. Box 49
Khartoum

SWEDEN
Natural Family Planning Centre
Dept of Medical Bio-physics
University of Umea
901—87 Umea

TAHITI
Convent of Our Lady of the
  Angels
BP 392
Papeete

TANZANIA
Sr Dr Birgitta Schnell
St Benedict's Hospital
Box 1003, Ndana via Lindi
Mtwara Region

UGANDA
Family Life Program
Uganda Catholic Secretariat
P.O. Box 993
Mbale

Mrs Monica Barenzi
Uganda Catholic Secretariat
P.O. Box 2886
Kampala

UKRAINE
Dr Antonius Ljavinetz
Saksagankogo 90/137
252–032 Kiev

URUGUAY
Centro Nacional de Planificacion
   Natural de la Familia
Pablo de Maria 1362
11200 Montevideo

USA
BOMA USA
Ms Sue Ek, Executive Director
PO Box 16206
St Paul MN 55116

TeenSTAR
8514 Bradmoor Drive
Bethesda
Maryland 20817-3810

Spanish-speaking:

Maria R. Garcia
Family Ministries
Archdiocese of Chicago
155 E Superior Street
Chicago IL 60611

VENEZUELA
AVEMO Billings
   Planificacion Natural de la
   Familia Centro National
Apt. do 80505
Prados del Este Caracas
Venezuela 1080

ZIMBABWE
Christian Health Care
PO Box 4024
Bulawayo

References

Chapter 2 THE MUCUS DISCOVERY

1. W. T. Pommerenke, *American Journal of Obstetrics and Gynecology*, 52: 1023, 1946.
2. E. Rydberg, *Acta. Obstet. Gynec. Scand.*, 29 (facs. 1): 127, 1948.
3. M. A. Breckenridge and W. T. Pommerenke, 'Analysis of carbohydrates in human cervical mucus', *Fertility and Sterility*, 2: 29, 1952.
4. M. R. Cohen, I. F. Stein and B. M. Kaye, *Fertility and Sterility*, 3: 202, 1952.
5. W. T. Smith, *The Pathology and Treatment of Leucorrhoea*, Churchill, London, 1855.
6. J. M. Sims, *British Medical Journal*, 2: 465–92, 1868.
7. M. Huhner, *Sterility in Male–Female and its Treatment*, Redman Co., New York, 1913.
8. J. Seguy and H. Simmonet, *Gynec. et Obstet.*, 28: 657, 1933.

Chapter 3 GETTING TO KNOW YOUR MENSTRUAL CYCLE

1. A. E. Treloar, R. E. Boynton, B. G. Behn, G. B. Borghild, B. W. Brown, 'Variation of the human menstrual cycle through reproductive life', *International Journal of Fertility*, 12: 77–126, 1970.
2. E. Odeblad, *Teacher-training Manual of Natural Family Planning*, University of Umea, Sweden, 1991.

Chapter 4 THE KEY TO FERTILITY CONTROL—THE MUCUS

1. E. L. Billings, J. J. Billings, J. B. Brown, H. G. Burger, 'Symptoms and hormonal changes accompanying ovulation', *Lancet*, 1: 282–4, 1972.
2. C. G. Hartman, *Science and the Safe Period*, The Williams and Wilkins Co., Baltimore, 1962, pp. 69–71.

Chapter 7   QUESTIONS OFTEN ASKED

1.   Dr (Sr) Leonie McSweeney, Report to VIth International Institute of the Ovulation Method, Los Angeles, 1980.
2.   T. W. Hilgers, Report to the VIth International Institute of the Ovulation Method, Los Angeles, 1980.
3.   E. L. Billings, Study of Pre-Menopausal Women, Report to Workshop of the Ovulation Method, Sydney, 1973.
4.   H. Klaus et al., 'Use effectiveness and client satisfaction in six centres teaching the Billings Ovulation Method', *Contraception*, 19: 6, 613, 1979.
5.   S. Thapa, M. V. Wonga, P. G. Lampe, H. Pietojo, A. Soejoenoes, 'Efficacy of Three Variations of Periodic Abstinence for Family Planning Indonesia', *Studies in Family Planning*, 21: 327–34, 1990.
6.   Indian Council of Medical Research, *Optimism with Natural Family Planning for Fertility Regulation in India*, Preliminary Report of a Five-state Study of the B.O.M. in India, 1986 to 1988. Presented at the Conference on the Welfare of Women, St John's College Hospital, Bangalore, India, January 1990.
7.   S. Z. Qian, D. W. Zhang, H. Z. Zuo, R. K. Lu, L. Peng and C. H. He, 'Evaluation of the Effectiveness of a Natural Fertility Regulation Programme in China', *Bulletin of the Ovulation Method Research and Reference Centre of Australia*, Vol. 27, No. 4, 2000.

Chapter 8   LEARNING ABOUT FERTILITY IN ADOLESCENCE

1.   UK National Case-control Study Group, 'Oral Contraceptive Use and Breast Cancer Ca.—Risk in Young Women', *Lancet*, 973–82, May 1989.
2.   D. R. Mishell, 'Contraception', in S. S. C. Yen, R. B. Jaffe and R. L. Barbieri (eds), *Reproductive Endocrinology*, W. B. Saunders, Philadelphia, 1999, p. 689.
3.   *Handbook on sexually transmitted diseases*, National Health and Medical Research Council (Australia), April 1977.

Chapter 9   COMING OFF THE PILL

1.   Editorial, 'Amenorrhoea after oral contraceptives', *British Medical Journal*, 18 September 1976, pp. 660–1.
2.   E. Odeblad, *Teacher-training Manual of the Billings Method*, University of Umea, Sweden, 1991.
3.   U.S. Food and Drug Administration, detailed patient labelling leaflet on contraception, April 1978.

Chapter 10 BREASTFEEDING AND THE BILLINGS METHOD

1.   J. W. Cox, 'Australia and New Zealand', *Jn. Obs-Gyn*, 19: 7, 1979.
2.   Toddywaller, *American Journal of Obstetrics and Gynecology*, 127–245, 1977.
3.   N. Leach, scientist and teacher, Ovulation Method Advisory Service, Dublin, Ireland, personal communication.
4.   R. Short, director, Medical Research Council, Unit of Reproductive Biology, Edinburgh, personal communication.
5.   WHO Task Force on Oral Contraception, 'Effects of Hormonal Contraceptives on Breast Milk Composition and Infant Growth', *Stud. Fam. Plann.*, 19 (6 Pt 1): 361–9, Nov.–Dec. 1988.
6.   J. B. Brown, 'Urinary Excretion of Oestrogen During Pregnancy, Lactation and the Re-establishment of Menstruation, *Lancet*, 1: 704, 1956.
7.   B. A. Gross and C. J. Eastman, 'Prolactin and the Return of Ovulation in Breastfeeding Women', *J. Biosoc. Sci.*, Suppl. 9: 25, 1985.
8.   P. R. Lewis, J. B. Brown, M. B. Renfree, R. V. Short, 'The Resumption of Ovulation and Menstruation in a Well-Nourished Population of Women Breastfeeding for an Extended Period of Time', *Fertility and Sterility*, Vol. 55, 3: 529–36, Mar. 1991.
9.   J. B. Brown, Professor of Obstetrics and Gynaecology, University of Melbourne, Organon Lecture, Sydney, 1 September 1978.
10. ibid.

Chapter 11 APPROACHING THE MENOPAUSE

1.   World Health Organisation, *Research on the Menopause in the 1990s*, WHO Technical Report, Series 866, 1996, p. 31.
2.   L. Dennerstein, G. Burrows, L. Cox, C. Wood, *Gynaecology, Sex and Psyche*, Melbourne University Press, Melbourne, 1978, p. 167.
3.   E. L. Billings, Report to Workshop on the Ovulation Method, Sydney, 1973.
4.   C. Schairer, J. Lubin et al., 'Menopausal estrogen and estrogen-progestin replacement therapy and breast cancer risk', *Journal of the American Medical Association*, 283, 2000, pp. 485–91; R. K. Ross, A. Paganini-Hill et al., 'Effect of hormone replacement therapy on breast cancer: estrogen versus estrogen plus progestin', *Journal of the National Cancer Institute*, 92, 2000, pp. 328–32; Writing Group for the Women's Health Initiative Investigators, 'Risks and Benefits of Estrogen Plus Progestin in Healthy Postmenopausal Women: Principal Results from the Women's Health Initiative Randomized Controlled Trial', *Journal of the American Medical Association*, 288, 2002, pp. 321–33.

5. S. W. Fletcher and G. A. Colditz, Editorial, 'Failure of Estrogen Plus Progestin Therapy for Prevention', *Journal of the American Medical Association*, 288, 2002, pp. 366–8.
6. K. Little, *Bone Behaviour*, Academic Press, London and New York, 1973, pp. 301–8.
7. The Royal Australasian College of Physicians, Working Group, *Osteoporosis —Its Causes, Preventions and Treatment*, 1990.
8. P. D. Delmas, 'Treatment of postmenopausal osteoporosis', *Lancet*, 359, 2002, pp. 2018–26; S. R. Cummings, S. Eckert et al., 'The effect of raloxifene on risk of breast cancer in postmenopausal women', *Journal of the American Medical Association*, 281, 1999, pp. 2189–97.

Chapter 12   DIFFICULTIES IN CONCEIVING

1. R. L. Barbieri, 'Infertility' in S. S. C. Yen, R. B. Jaffe and R. B. Barbieri, *Reproductive Endocrinology: Physiology, Pathophysiology, and Clinical Management*, W. B. Saunders Co., 1999, pp. 573–4.
2. R. W. Rebar, 'Practical Evaluation of Hormonal Status' in S. S. C. Yen et al., op. cit., p. 709.
3. E. Odeblad, *Teacher-training Manual of Natural Family Planning*, University of Umea, Sweden, 1991.
4. J. A. Collins 'Unexplained infertility' in W. R. Keye, R. J. Chang et al. (eds) *Infertility: Evaluation and Treatment*, W. B. Saunders Co., 1995, pp. 249–62.
5. WHO Scientific Group, *Recent Advances in Medically Assisted Conception*, WHO Technical Report Series 820, 1992.
6. M. Pugeat, P. H. Ducluzeau, 'Insulin resistance, polycystic ovary syndrome and metformin', *Drugs*, 58, 1999.
7. K. A. Awartini, A. P. Cheung, 'Metformin and polycystic ovary syndrome: a literature review', *Journal of Obstetrics and Gynaecology Canada*, 24(5), 2002, pp. 393–401.
8. S. A. Arslanian, V. Lewy, K. Danadian, R. Saad, ' Metformin therapy in obese adolescents with polycystic ovary syndrome and impaired glucose tolerance: amelioration of exaggerated adrenal response to adrenocorticotropin with reduction of insulinemia/insulin resistance', *Journal of Clinical Endocrinology & Metabolism* 87(4), 2002, pp. 1555–9.
9. R. L. Barbieri, op. cit., p. 574.
10. W. C. Scott, 'Pelvic abscess in association with intrauterine contraceptive device', *American Journal of Obstetrics and Gynecology*, 131: 149–56, 1978.
11. T. M. Farley, M. J. Rosenberg, P. J. Rowe et al., 'Intrauterine devices and pelvic inflammatory disease: An international perspective', *Lancet*, 339, 1992, p. 785.

12. M. A. Khatamee, 'T-Mycoplasma in abortion and infertility', *The Female Patient*, 109–12, October 1978.

13. G. Howe et al., 'Effects of Age, Cigarette Smoking and Other Factors in Fertility' (findings in a large prospective study), *British Medical Journal*, 290: 1697–1700, 1985.

14. W. Winkelstein, Jr, 'Smoking and Cervical Cancer—Current Status' (a review), *American Journal of Epidemiology*, 31 (6): 945–57, 1991.

15. R. L. Barbieri, op. cit., pp. 582–3.

16. T. Hurst, P. Lancaster, *Assisted conception Australia and New Zealand 1999 and 2000*. AIHW Cat. No. PER 18, Australian Institute of Health and Welfare National Perinatal Statistics Unit (Assisted Conception Series No. 6) 2001, pp. 11–12.

17. R. L. Barbieri, op. cit., p. 571.

18. Hurst et al., op. cit., p. 19.

19. ibid., pp. 23–5.

20. Victorian Infertility Treatment Authority, *Annual Report 2001*, p. 20.

21. R. W. Rebar, op. cit., pp. 715–16; S. P. Buyers, 'Evaluation and treatment of disorders of the cervix' in W. R. Keye, R. J. Chang et al. (eds), *Infertility: Evaluation and Treatment*, W. B. Saunders Co., 1995, pp. 195–229.

22. D. Blake, D. Smith, M. Bargiacchi, G. Gudex, 'Fertility Awareness of Women Attending Fertility Clinic', *Australia and New Zealand Journal of Obstetrics and Gynaecology*, 1997, 37(3), p. 350.

23. J. B. Stanford, G. L. White, H. Hatasaka, 'Timing intercourse to achieve pregnancy: Current evidence', *Obstetrics and Gynaecology*, 2002, 100(6), pp. 1333–41.

Chapter 13 THE TECHNOLOGICAL APPROACH TO CONTRACEPTION

1. International Medical Advisory Panel of the International Planned Parenthood Federation, 'Statement on steroidal oral contraception', *Healthright*, Vol. 6, No. 4, August 1987.

2. Dr Malcolm Potts, Family Health International, address to Fifth Advanced Course in Obstetrics and Care of the Newborn, Royal Women's Hospital, Melbourne, 22 July 1991.

3. L. Potter and M. Williams-Deane, 'The importance of oral contraceptive compliance', *International Planned Parenthood Federation Bulletin*, 24: 5, October 1990.

4. ibid, p. 2.

5. International Medical Advisory Panel, op. cit.

6. World Health Organisation, 'Collaborative study of cardiovascular disease and steroid hormone contraception. Ischaemic stroke and

combined oral contraceptives: results of an international, multicentre, case-control study', *Lancet*, 348, 1996, pp. 498–505; World Health Organisation, 'Collaborative Study of Cardiovascular Disease and Steroid Hormone Contraception. Acute myocardial infarction and combined oral contraceptives: results of an international, multicentre, case-control study', *Lancet*, 349, 1997, pp. 1202–09.

7.   D. C. G. Skegg, 'Third generation oral contraceptives. Caution is still justified', *British Medical Journal*, 321, 2000, pp. 190–1.

8.   International Medical Advisory Panel, op. cit.

9.   K. Little, *Bone Behaviour*, Academic Press, London and New York, 1973, pp. 284–7.

10.   Editorial, 'Thrombo-embolism and oral contraceptives', *British Medical Journal*, 213, 19 February 1974.

11.   K. Bloemenkamp, F. Rosendall et al., 'Enhancement by factor V Leiden mutation of risk of deep-vein thrombosis associated with oral contraceptives containing a third-generation progestogen', *Lancet*, 346, 1995, pp. 1593–6.

12.   H. Jick, S. S. Jick et al., 'Risk of idiopathic cardiovascular death and nonfatal venous thromboembolism in women using oral contraceptives with differing progestogen components', *Lancet*, 346, 1995, pp. 1589–93.

13.   W. Spitzer, M. A. Lewis et al., 'Third generation oral contraceptives and risk of venous thromboembolic disorders: an international case-control study', *British Medical Journal*, 312, 1996, pp. 83–8.

14.   World Health Organisation, 'Collaborative study in cardiovascular disease and steroid hormone contraception. Effect of different progestogens in low dose oral contraceptives on venous thromboembolic disease', *Lancet*, 346, 1995, pp. 1582–93.

15.   P. A. O'Brien, 'The third generation oral contraceptive controversy', *British Medical Journal*, 319, 1999, pp. 795–6.

16.   L. Mellemkjaer, H. T. Sorensen et al., 'Admission for and mortality from primary venous thromboembolism in women of fertile age in Denmark, 1977–95', *British Medical Journal*, 319, 1999, pp. 820–1.

17.   D. C. Skegg, op. cit., pp. 190–1.

18.   J. P. Vandenbroucke, F. M. Helmerhorst et al., 'Competing interests and controversy about third generation oral contraceptives', *British Medical Journal*, 320, 2000, pp. 381–2.

19.   J. M. Kemmeren, A. Algra et al., 'Third generation oral contraceptives and risk of venous thrombosis: meta-analysis', *British Medical Journal*, 323, 2001, pp. 131–4.

20.   International Medical Advisory Panel, op. cit.

21.   H. Klonoff-Cohen, D. Savitz, R. Cefalo, M. McCann, 'An Epidemiologic Study of Contraception and Preeclampsia', *Journal of the American Medical Association*, Vol. 262, No. 22, 8 Dec. 1989.

22. World Health Organisation, 'Collaborative Study of Cardiovascular Disease and Steroid Hormone Contraception. Ischaemic stroke and combined oral contraceptives: results of an international, multicentre, case-control study', *Lancet*, 348, 1996, pp. 498–505.

23. International Medical Advisory Panel, op. cit.

24. E. Weisberg, 'Questions Women Ask About the Pill, *Australian Prescriber*, 2: 3, 56, 1978.

25. D. R. Mishell, 'Contraception' in S. S. C. Yen, R. B. Jaffe and R. L. Barbieri (eds), op. cit., pp. 690–1.

26. ibid, p. 690.

27. E. C. G. Grant, C. M. Steel et al., 'Medical profession needs to examine facts', *British Medical Journal*, 319, 1999, p. 387.

28. J. Horowitz, 'Relative risk of liver cancer remains high', *British Medical Journal*, 319, 1999, p. 386.

29. US Food and Drug Administration, detailed patient labelling leaflet on contraception, April 1978.

30. World Health Organisation, 'Task Force on Oral Contraceptives', *Studies in Family Planning*, 19, 1988, pp. 361–9.

31. P. Lukko, R. Erkkola et al., 'Ectopic pregnancies during use of low-dose progestogens for oral contraception', *Contraception*, 16, 1977, pp. 575–80.

32. J. Coste, N. Job-Spira et al., 'Risk factors for ectopic pregnancy: a case-control study in France, with special focus on infectious factors', *American Journal of Epidemiology*, 133, 1991, pp. 839–49.

33. J. I. Tay, J. Moore et al., 'Ectopic pregnancy', *British Medical Journal*, 320, 2000, pp. 916–19.

34. J. J. Schlesselman, 'Net effect of oral contraceptive use on the risk of cancer in women in the United States', *Obstetrics and Gynecology*, 85, 1995, p. 793.

35. World Health Organisation, op. cit., pp. 361–9.

36. E. Stern, A. B. Forsythe, L. Youkeles et al., 'Steroid contraceptive use and cervical dysplasia: increased risk of progression', *Science*, 196: 1460, 1977.

37. Collaborative Group on Hormonal Factors in Breast Cancer, 'Breast cancer and hormonal contraceptives: Collaborative reanalysis of individual data on 53,297 women with breast cancer and 100,239 women without breast cancer from 54 epidemiological studies', *Lancet*, 347, 1996, p. 1713.

38. Collaborative Group on Hormonal Factors in Breast Cancer, 'Breast cancer and hormonal contraceptives: Further results', *Contraception*, 54, 1996, pp. S1–S106.

39. D. R. Mishell, op. cit., p. 684.

40. 'Oral contraception proceedings of seminar, Adelaide, Australia', supplement in *Australian Family Physician*, 8–11 March 1977.

41. D. R. Mishell, op. cit., p. 688.

42. Collaborative Group on Hormonal Factors in Breast Cancer, op. cit., Further results.

43. International Medical Advisory Panel, op. cit.

44. ibid.

45. Weisberg, op. cit., p. 57.

46. F. J. Kane, 'Evaluation of emotional reactions to oral contraceptive use', *American Journal of Obstetrics and Gynecology*, 12: 6, 968–71, 1976.

47. D. R. Mishell, op. cit., p. 683.

48. C. Djerassi, *Science*, 248: 1061, 1990.

49. 'Natural family planning in today's world', *Research in Reproduction*, Vol. 22, No. 3, July 1990.

50. A. Szarewski and J. Guillebaud, 'Contraception: current state of the art', *British Medical Journal*, Vol. 302, 25 May 1991, p. 1225.

51. *Guidelines for the use of Intrauterine Contraceptive Devices. Report of the National Health and Medical Research Council's expert panel on women's health.* Approved by the NHMRC, June 1989, p. 2.

52. Szarewski and Guillebaud, op. cit., p. 1225.

53. *Guidelines (NHMRC)*, op. cit., p. 2.

54. ibid.

55. D. R. Mishell, op. cit., pp. 702–3.

56. T. M. Farley, M. J. Rosenberg et al., 'Intrauterine devices and pelvic inflammatory disease: An international perspective', *Lancet*, 339, 1992, pp. 785–7.

57. E. Persson, K. Homberg et al., '*Actinomyces israelii* in genital tract of women with and without intrauterine contraceptive devices', *Acta Obstetrics and Gynecology Scandinavia 62*, 1983, pp. 563–5.

58. NHMRC, *Guidelines*, op. cit., p. 4.

59. *Contraceptive Technology*, 17, 1, 1996, pp. 13–24.

60. ibid.

61. ibid

62. US Food and Drug Administration, op. cit.

63. Shearman, op. cit.

64. US Department of Health and Human Services report, 2001.

65. J. Trussell, K. Sturgen et al., 'Comparative contraceptive efficacy of the female condom and other barrier methods', *Family Planning Perspectives*, 26, 1994, pp. 66–8.

66. WHO Task Force on long-acting systemic agents for fertility regulation, 'Microdose intravaginal levonorgestrel contraception: a multicentre clinical trial', *Contraception* 41: 105–67, 1990.

67. *Contraceptive Technology*, op. cit.

68. D. R. Mishell, op. cit., p. 696.

69. C. Westhoff, 'Depomedroxyprogesterone acetate contraception. Metabolic parameters and mood changes', *Journal of Reproductive Medicine*, 41 (suppl), 1996, pp. 401–4.

70. L. L. Moore, R. Valuck et al., 'A comparative study of one-year weight gain among users of medroxyprogesterone acetate, levonorgestrel implants, and oral contraceptives', *Contraception*, 52, 1995, pp. 215–18.

71. ibid., p. 694.

72. F. C. Reader, 'Emergency contraception', *British Medical Journal*, Vol. 302, 6 April 1991.

73. J. Trussell, C. Ellertson et al., 'The effectiveness of the Yuzpe regimen of emergency contraception', *Family Planning Perspectives*, 28, 1996, pp. 58–61.

74. Task Force on Postovulatory Methods of Fertility Regulation, 'Randomised controlled trial of levonorgestrel versus Yuzpe regimen of combined oral contraceptives for emergency contraception', *Lancet*, 352, 1998, pp. 428–33.

75. L. Cheng, A. M. Gulmezoglu et al., 'Interventions for emergency contraception (Cochrane Review)', *Cochrane Library*, Issue 2, Oxford: Update Software, 2000.

76. J. Guillebaud, 'Medical termination of pregnancy', *British Medical Journal*, Vol. 301, 18–25 August 1990.

77. ibid, p. 353.

78. World Health Organisation, Task Force on Methods for the Regulation of Male Fertility, 'Contraceptive efficacy of testosterone-induced azoospermia in normal men', *Lancet*, 335, p. 955.

79. World Health Organisation, Task Force on Methods for the Regulation of Male Fertility, 'Rates of testosterone-induced suppression to severe oligozoospermia or azoospermia in two multicentre clinical studies', *International Journal of Andrology*, 18, 1995, pp. 157–65.

80. World Health Organisation, Task Force on Methods for the Regulation of Male Fertility, 'Contraceptive efficacy of testosterone-induced azoospermia and oligozoospermia in normal men', *Fertility and Sterility*, 65, 1996, pp. 81–9.

81. ESHRE Capri Workshop, op. cit., p. 368.

82. D. R. Mishell, op. cit., pp. 699–700.

83. Guillebaud, op. cit., p. 1225.

Chapter 14 NATURAL METHODS

1.   US Food and Drug Administration, detailed patient labelling leaflet on contraception, April 1978.

2.   H. Burger, 'The Ovulation Method of fertility regulation', *Modern Medicine in Australia*, 39, April 1978.

3. J. J. Billings, *The Ovulation Method*, Advocate Press, Melbourne, 1980.

4. H. Shapiro, *The Birth Control Book*, Avon, New York, 1978, p. 128.

Chapter 15 SCIENTIFIC BACKGROUND OF THE METHOD

1. J. B. Brown, 'The scientific basis of the Ovulation Method', in J. J. Billings et al., *The Billings Atlas of the Ovulation Method*, 5th edition, 1989. Ovulation Method Research & Reference Centre of Australia, Melbourne.

2. E. L. Billings, J. J. Billings, J. B. Brown, H. C. Burger, 'Symptoms and hormonal changes accompanying ovulation', *Lancet* I: 282–4, 1972.

3. A. M. Flynn and S. S. Lynch, 'Cervical mucus and identification of the fertile phase of the menstrual cycle', *British Journal of Obstetrics and Gynaecology*, 83, 656, 1976.

4. J. H. Casey, 'The Correlation between Mid-cycle Hormonal Profiles, Cervical Mucus and Ovulation in Normal Women', in *Human Love and Human Life*, Polding Press, Melbourne, 1979, p. 68.

5. S. Cortesi, G. Rigoni, F. Zen, R. Sposetti, 'Correlation of plasma gonadatrophins and ovarian steroids pattern with symptomatic changes in cervical mucus during the menstrual cycle in normal cycling women', *Contraception*, 23: 6, 629, June 1981.

6. T. W. Hilgers, G. Abraham, D. Cavanagh, 'The Peak symptom and estimated time of ovulation', *Natural Family Planning*, Vol. 52. No. 5, November 1978.

7. Ovulation Method Research and Reference Centre of Australia, 'Studies on human reproduction, ovarian activity and fertility, and the Billings Ovulation Method', July 2000.

8. WHO Colloquium, 'The Cervical Mucus in Human Reproduction', Geneva, 1972.

9. E. Odeblad, A. Hoglund et al., 'The dynamic mosaic model of the human ovulatory cervical mucus', Proc. Nord. Fert. Soc. Meeting, Umea, January 1978.

10. E. Odeblad, *Teacher-training Manual of Natural Family Planning*, University of Umea, Sweden, 1991.

11. Odeblad, ibid.

12. J. J. Billings, *The Ovulation Method*, Advocate Press, Melbourne, 7th edition, 1983.

13. S. J. Thornton, R. J. Pepperell, J. B. Brown, 'Home Monitoring of gonadotropin ovulation induction using the Ovarian Monitor', *Fertility and Sterility*, 1990, 54: 1076–82.

14. C. Cavero, 'Using an ovarian monitor as an adjunct to natural family planning', *Journal of Nurse-Midwifery*, 1995, 40: 269–76.

Chapter 16 TRIALS OF THE METHOD

1. Bernard G. Greenberg, 'Method Effectiveness Evaluation', *Natural Family Planning*, Human Life Foundation, 284, 1973.

2. R. G. Potter, 'Application of life table techniques to measurements of contraceptive effectiveness', *Demography*, 3, 299, 1966.

3. C. Tietze and S. Lewit, *Family Planning Perspectives*, 3, 53, 1971.

4. M. C. Weissman, J. Foliaki, E. L. Billings, J. J. Billings, 'A trial of the Ovulation Method of family planning in Tonga', *Lancet*, 813–16, 14 October 1972.

5. S. Z. Qian, D. W. Zhang, H. Z. Zuo, R. K. Lu, L. Peng, C. H. He, 'Evaluation of the Effectiveness of a Natural Fertility Regulation Programme in China', reprinted from *Bulletin of the Ovulation Method Research and Reference Centre of Australia*, 2000, Vol. 27, No. 4, pp. 17–22.

6. M. Ball, 'A prospective field trial of the Ovulation Method', *European Journal of Obstetrical and Gynaecological Reproductive Biology*, 6/2, 63–6, 1976.

7. E. L. Billings, Report to Workshop on the Ovulation Method, Sydney, 1973.

8. Kyo Sang Cho, Report to World Health Organisation Conference, Geneva, February 1976.

9. C. B. Haliburn, Report to VIth International Institute of the Ovulation Method, Los Angeles, 1980.

10. Indian Council of Medical Research, 'Optimism With Natural Family Planning for Fertility Regulation in India', preliminary report of a five state study of the B. O. M. in India 1986 to 1988, presented at the Conference on the Welfare of Women, St John's College Hospital, Bangalore, India, January 1990. *Contraception*, 53: 69–74, 1996.

11. N. Leach, Ovulation Method Advisory Service, Dublin, personal communication.

12. M. F. Wade et al., 'A randomised prospective study of the use effectiveness of two methods of natural family planning: an interim report', *American Journal of Obstetrics and Gynecology*, 134, 628, 1979.

13. H. Klaus et al., 'Use effectiveness and client satisfaction in six centres teaching the Billings Ovulation Method', *Contraception*, 19: 6, 613, 1979.

14. Minister of Health and Social Action of Burkina Faso, *Bulletin d'Epidemiol. et d'Inform.* Socio. -Sanitaire, No. 17, 1990.

15. S. Thapa, M. V. Wonga, P. G. Lampe, H. Pietojo, A. Soejoenoes, 'Efficacy of Three Variations of Periodic Abstinence for Family Planning in Indonesia', *Studies in Family Planning*, 21: 327–34, 1990.

16. World Health Organisation, Task Force on Methods for the Determination of the Fertile Period, Special Programme of Research,

Development and Research Training in Human Reproduction, 'A Prospective Multicentre Trial of the Ovulation Method of Natural Family Planning. I. The Teaching Phase', *Fertility and Sterility*, 36, 152, 1981.

17. S. Z. Qian, D. W. Zhang et al., op. cit.

Glossary

ADHESION   A fibrous band of tissue that abnormally binds or interconnects organs or other body parts.

AIDS   Acquired immune deficiency syndrome.

AMENORRHOEA   The prolonged absence of menstruation.

ANOVULAR CYCLES   A term used when ovulation does not occur before bleeding. Anovular bleeding.

ANTIBIOTIC   A drug, for example penicillin, that is used to treat diseases caused by bacteria.

ANTIBODY   A protein produced by the body's immune (defence) system in response to an intruder. Antibodies serve to render intruders harmless.

ARTIFICIAL INSEMINATION   The depositing of semen in the vagina by means other than sexual intercourse.

BACTERIA   Single-celled organisms, some of which cause disease, while others are helpful to the body.

BASAL BODY TEMPERATURE (BBT)   The lowest normal body temperature recorded under conditions of absolute rest; taken immediately after waking and before rising.

BASIC INFERTILE PATTERN (BIP)   The pattern of discharge indicating relative inactivity of the ovaries before a follicle begins to mature.

BILLINGS METHOD   A technique of natural fertility control in which days of infertility, possible fertility, and maximum fertility are identified by a woman's observations of mucus at the vaginal opening.

CAUTERY   Burning of diseased tissue, for example the cervix. See also TUBAL CAUTERY.

CERVIX   The lower part of the uterus (womb) that projects into the vagina.

CHANGE OF LIFE   The CLIMACTERIC.

CHROMOSOME   One of the forty-six microscopic units within each cell that carries the genetic material responsible for inherited characteristics.

climacteric   The menopausal years, during which reproductive function ceases. (Sometimes referred to as 'the change' or 'change of life'.)

COLOSTRUM   The first milk from the mother's breasts.

COLPOSCOPY   The technique of viewing the cervix under magnification, using a colposcope.

CONCEIVE   To become pregnant.

CONCEPTION   The fusion of sperm and egg.

CONDOM   A sheath of rubber or plastic which is worn to prevent conception.

CORPUS LUTEUM   The yellow structure formed in the ovary after the release of an egg cell. If the egg is fertilised, the corpus luteum grows and produces hormones that support the pregnancy for several months. In the absence of fertilisation, it degenerates.

CRYOSURGERY   Surgery involving freezing of diseased tissue without significantly harming normal adjacent structures.

CURETTAGE   The scraping out of the lining of the uterus with an instrument called a curette.

CYST   Any sac-like structure containing fluid or semi-solid material.

DANAZOL   A synthetic medication similar in structure to the male hormone, testosterone, used for the treatment of endometriosis.

DEPO-PROVERA   A synthetic progesterone-like hormone used as a contraceptive.

DIAPHRAGM   A rubber, dome-shaped device worn over the cervix during intercourse to prevent conception.

DIATHERMY   A technique in which local heat is produced in the body tissues below the surface.

DILATATION AND CURETTAGE (D AND C)   A surgical procedure in which the cervix is gradually opened with instruments called dilators. Tissue is then removed from the surface of the endometrium and cervix with a curette.

DIXARIT   A non-hormonal medication used to treat hot flushes.

DOUCHE   A substance flushed through the vagina.

DYSPAREUNIA   Painful or difficult intercourse.

EARLY DAY RULES   The Billings Method guidelines for avoiding a pregnancy from the beginning of the cycle up to the Peak of the mucus system.

ECTOPIC PREGNANCY   A pregnancy that develops outside the normal location within the uterus. Ectopic pregnancies usually occur in the Fallopian tubes.

EGG CELL (OVUM)   The female cell that on fusion with a sperm cell forms a new individual.

EJACULATION   Discharge of semen from the penis.

EMBRYO   The initial stages in the formation of a baby.

ENDOCRINOLOGIST   A doctor who specialises in the function of hormones.

ENDOMETRIOSIS   A condition caused by the presence of pieces of the endometrium in areas other than the normal location, the uterus.

ENDOMETRIUM   The inner lining of the uterus.

ESTROGEN   See OESTROGEN.

ETHINYL OESTRADIOL   A form of oestrogen that is effective in producing cervical mucus with fertile characteristics.

FALLOPIAN TUBES   The muscular tubes (two) along which the embryo travels to the uterus, and in which the egg is fertilised.

FERNING   The fern-like pattern of L-mucus when dried on a glass slide.

FERTILE DAYS   The days of the menstrual cycle during which intercourse may result in pregnancy.

FERTILE SIGNS, MUCUS WITH   Mucus from the cervix which is produced close to the time of ovulation. It has a slippery, lubricative sensation, tends to form strings, and resembles raw egg-white.

FERTILISATION   The fusion of an egg and a sperm.

FERTILITY   The ability to reproduce.

FERTILITY DRUGS   A group of natural and synthetic substances capable of enabling some women to conceive.

FIBROID   A benign tumour in the wall of the uterus.

FOETUS   The developing baby from seven weeks to birth.

FOLLICLE   A small fluid-filled structure within the ovary that contains the developing egg. At ovulation, the egg is released when the follicle breaks through the surface of the ovary.

FOLLICLE STIMULATING HORMONE (FSH)   The hormone produced by the pituitary gland that stimulates the ovaries to produce mature egg cells and oestrogen hormone.

GENETIC   Having to do with hereditary characteristics.

GENITAL   Having reference to the organs of reproduction.

GENITAL CONTACT   Contact of the penis with the vaginal opening, or tissues around it.

GONORRHOEA   A highly contagious venereal disease.

GYNAECOLOGIST   A doctor who specialises in the treatment and management of problems affecting the female reproductive system.

HAEMORRHAGE   Excessively heavy bleeding.

HIV   Human immuno-deficiency virus causing AIDS.

HORMONE   A chemical substance produced within the body which stimulates or affects other organs or body parts.

HOT FLUSHES   Sudden flushing of the skin accompanied by perspiration and a feeling of intense heat.

HUHNER'S (POST-COITAL) TEST   Examination of the sperm in cervical mucus shortly after intercourse at peak fertility.

HYPOTHALAMUS   A major control centre of the body, situated at the base of the brain, and interacting with the pituitary gland.

HYSTERECTOMY   The surgical removal of the uterus and cervix.

HYSTEROSALPINGOGRAM   An X-ray taken after a special dye is injected through the cervix. It produces an image of the inside of the uterus and the Fallopian tubes.

IMPLANTATION   The embedding of the embryo in the lining of the uterus.

IMPOTENCE   The inability to obtain or maintain an erection of the penis.

INCOMPETENT CERVIX   A cervix that is too weak to carry the weight of a growing pregnancy.

INFERTILITY   Temporary or permanent inability to conceive or reproduce.

INTERCOURSE   Sexual relations involving the insertion of the penis into the vagina, with the release of sperm.

INTRAUTERINE DEVICE (IUD)   Any device placed within the uterus for the purpose of avoiding conception.

LACTATION   The production of milk by the breasts.

LAPAROSCOPY   A procedure in which the inside of the abdomen, and particularly the ovaries, is examined using an instrument like a thin telescope (called a laparoscope).

LAPAROTOMY   The surgical operation of opening the abdomen.

LIBIDO   Sex drive; the desire for sexual intercourse.

LOCHIA   The discharge from the uterus and vagina during the first few weeks after giving birth.

LUTEAL PHASE   Interval of time between ovulation and menstruation.

LUTEINISING HORMONE (LH)   A hormone from the pituitary gland in the brain that stimulates ovulation and the formation of the corpus luteum.

MASTURBATE   To obtain a sexual orgasm by self-manipulation of the genital organs.

MEMBRANE   Moist layer of cells that lines body cavities and passage-ways.

MENARCHE   The age at which vaginal bleeding begins.

MENOPAUSE   The permanent cessation of vaginal bleeding.

MENSTRUAL CYCLE   The time interval from the beginning of one menstrual cycle to the beginning of the next. During the cycle ovulation occurs and the endometrium develops, regresses and is shed.

MENSTRUATION   The period of bleeding from the uterus that occurs approximately monthly, 11–16 days after ovulation.

MINI PILL   A type of birth control Pill that contains a progestogen, but no oestrogen.

MUCUS, CERVICAL   The secretion from the lining cells of the cervix.

OBSTETRICIAN   A doctor who supervises pregnancy and childbirth.

OESTRADIOL   A type of oestrogen.

OESTROGEN   A hormone produced mainly in the ovaries that is responsible for female sexual characteristics and plays an important role in ovulation.

OSTEOPOROSIS   The loss of calcium and other substances from bone, leading to its softening and weakening.

OVARIAN CYCLE   A cyclic series of events occurring in the ovary during which an egg cell matures and is released.

OVARY   The female sex organ in which egg cells mature and hormones are produced which influence the release of the egg cells.

OVULATION   The release of an egg from the ovary.

OVULATION METHOD   See BILLINGS METHOD.

OVUM   See EGG CELL.

PEAK DAY   The last day of mucus with fertile characteristics in a menstrual cycle, which correlates closely with the time of ovulation.

PEAK RULE   The Billings Method guideline when the Peak is identified.

PEARL INDEX   A statistical measurement relating to pregnancies occurring among a trial group.

PELVIC INFLAMMATORY DISEASE   Inflammation and/or infection involving the internal female reproductive organs and pelvic tissues. Commonly used to describe any acute, recurrent or chronic infection of the Fallopian tubes and/or ovaries.

PENETRATION   The insertion of the penis into the vagina.

PENIS   The male organ, inserted into the vagina during intercourse.

PERFORATED UTERUS   A uterus in which the wall has been pierced, often inadvertently.

PITUITARY GLAND   The gland at the base of the brain that produces many important hormones, including those essential for reproduction.

POLYCYSTIC OVARIES   A condition in which the ovaries are studded with many small cysts.

POLYP   A small growth, shaped like a tear-drop, often found in the cervix or endometrium.

POSTCOITAL TEST   See HUHNER'S TEST.

PROGESTERONE   The female hormone produced by the corpus luteum as a result of ovulation. It supports the developing pregnancy.

PROGESTOGEN   A synthetic drug that has similar action to progesterone but which has troublesome side effects.

PROLACTIN   A hormone from the pituitary gland which stimulates breast milk production.

PROSTAGLANDINS   Naturally occurring substances capable of stimulating the muscular contractions of the uterus.

PUBERTY   The time of life in boys and girls when the reproductive organs become functional.

SEMEN   The fluid ejaculated by a man during intercourse or masturbation; contains sperm.

SPERM   The male reproductive cell which on fusing with an egg cell forms a new individual.

SPERMICIDAL   Destructive to sperm.

SPERMICIDES   Vaginal creams, foams, jellies, or suppositories that can immobilise or destroy sperm.

STD   Sexually transmitted disease.

STERILISATION   A procedure to render an individual permanently unable to reproduce.

STERILITY   The inability to conceive.

TESTES (TESTICLES)   Male sex organs in which sperm and the hormone testosterone are produced.

THROMBOSIS   A condition in which a plug or clot of blood partly or completely blocks a blood vessel.

TUBAL CAUTERY   The sealing of the Fallopian tubes by burning, rendering them impassable to sperm and egg cells; a form of sterilisation.

TUBAL LIGATION   Surgical sterilisation by tying a surgical string around a segment of the Fallopian tubes, thus preventing the egg and sperm from meeting.

TUBAL PREGNANCY   An ectopic pregnancy occurring in a Fallopian tube.

ULTRASOUND   A diagnostic technique which uses sound waves to produce an image of internal body structures.

UTERUS   The hollow muscular organ of reproduction in which the embryo implants and develops.

VAGINA   The female organ or passage into which sperm are released during intercourse.

VAGINISMUS   A painful spasm of the vagina which prevents penetration by the penis.

VASECTOMY   A surgical sterilisation procedure in which the vas deferens (the tube that carries sperm from the testes) is cut, and the ends separated, so that sperm can no longer pass through.

VENEREAL DISEASE (VD)   Any infection that is transmitted mainly by sexual intercourse.

WITHDRAWAL (COITUS INTERRUPTUS)   Sexual intercourse in which the penis is withdrawn and semen discharged outside the vagina.

WITHDRAWAL BLEEDING   Bleeding from the uterus following removal of hormonal support, for example the first bleeding after coming off the Pill.

ZYGOTE   The fertilised egg, the embryo.

Index

Personal record chart

	1	2	3	4	5	6	7	8	9	10	11	12	13	14	15	16	17	18	19	20	21	22	23	24	25	26	27	28	29	30	31	32	33	34	35
DATE / /																																			
MUCUS Sensation																																			
Appearance																																			
DATE / /																																			
MUCUS Sensation																																			
Appearance																																			
DATE / /																																			
MUCUS Sensation																																			
Appearance																																			
DATE / /																																			
MUCUS Sensation																																			
Appearance																																			
DATE / /																																			
MUCUS Sensation																																			
Appearance																																			

Personal record chart

	1	2	3	4	5	6	7	8	9	10	11	12	13	14	15	16	17	18	19	20	21	22	23	24	25	26	27	28	29	30	31	32	33	34	35
DATE / /																																			
MUCUS Sensation Appearance																																			
DATE / /																																			
MUCUS Sensation Appearance																																			
DATE / /																																			
MUCUS Sensation Appearance																																			
DATE / /																																			
MUCUS Sensation Appearance																																			
DATE / /																																			
MUCUS Sensation Appearance																																			

DR EVELYN BILLINGS, AM, DCSG, MBBS (Melb.), DCH (Lond.), completed her medical degree at the University of Melbourne and then trained as a specialist paediatrician. In 1966 she joined her husband, Dr John Billings, in his research on the Billings Ovulation Method, to which her studies on breastfeeding mothers and women approaching the menopause have made a major contribution. Dr Billings has written numerous articles in scientific journals and is co-author of the *Atlas of the Ovulation Method*. She and her husband travel widely each year, with an Australian teaching team.

ANN WESTMORE, PhD (Melb.), received her scientific training at the University of Melbourne, specialising in physiology and histology. She then joined the *Herald Sun* and became the medical and science writer. In 1977 she won the AMA's award for the best five medical news stories, in 1980 she won an AMA merit award for feature writing, and in 1998 she received a high commendation in the Royal Australian College of Ophthalmologists' Media Award. In 2002 she completed a PhD on the history of mid-twentieth-century Australian psychiatry.